ESSENTIAL HISTORIES

The War of 1812

Carl Benn

OSPREY PUBLISHING
Bloomsbury Publishing Plc
Kemp House, Chawley Park, Cumnor Hill, Oxford OX2 9PH, UK
29 Earlsfort Terrace, Dublin 2, Ireland
1385 Broadway, 5th Floor, New York, NY 10018, USA
E-mail: info@ospreypublishing.com
www.ospreypublishing.com

OSPREY is a trademark of Osprey Publishing Ltd

First published in Great Britain in 2024

© Osprey Publishing Ltd, 2024

The text in this edition is revised and updated from: ESS 41: *The War of 1812*
(Osprey Publishing, 2002).

Essential Histories Series Editor: Professor Robert O'Neill

A catalogue record for this book is available from the British Library.

ISBN: PB 9781472858566;
eBook 9781472858535;
ePDF 9781472858542;
XML 9781472858559;
Audio 9781472858573

24 25 26 27 28   10 9 8 7 6 5 4 3 2 1

For legal purposes the Acknowledgements on
p. 141 constitute an extension of this copyright page.

Cover design by Stewart Larking
Maps by The Map Studio, revised by www.bounford.com
Index by Alan Rutter
Typeset by PDQ Digital Media Solutions, Bungay, UK
Printed and bound in India by Replika Press Private Ltd.

Osprey Publishing supports the Woodland Trust, the UK's leading woodland
conservation charity.

To find out more about our authors and books visit www.ospreypublishing.com.
Here you will find extracts, author interviews, details of forthcoming events and
the option to sign up for our newsletter.

CONTENTS

INTRODUCTION

In the western parts of the lower Great Lakes and the upper Mississippi River in 1805, two Shawnee men, Tecumseh and Tenskwatawa, spoke words of enraged bitterness and religious revitalization to encourage the First Nations to form a defensive alliance. Their communities had lived through decades of profound dislocation, especially since the birth of the United States of America in 1776, as its citizens seemed to hold their rights in contempt when they conflicted with those of land-hungry settlers. Peaceful attempts to protect Indigenous interests had failed, and many people now thought they might have to fight in order to secure a future for their children.

Off the coast of Virginia two years later, during Great Britain's long war with France and its allies, the captain of HMS *Leopard* ordered the United States frigate *Chesapeake* to stop so he could search it for deserters from the Royal Navy. The Americans refused. The British fired a broadside, killing or wounding 21 men. After replying with a single shot to assert the dignity of the flag, the *Chesapeake* surrendered, whereupon a boarding party seized four deserters from the US vessel – one Briton and three Americans. This attack on a neutral warship outraged Americans, insulted their sovereignty, and served as a blunt symbol of the gravity of a wider crisis unfolding between the two countries over free trade and sailors' rights.

As relations between Great Britain and the United States degenerated towards war, many Americans wanted to seize the British provinces on their northern border. They hoped to retaliate for Britain's behaviour on the world's oceans, realize their dreams for America's destiny, and, for some, to profit personally. Others, such as James Madison, who became president in 1809, believed that conquest was desirable partly because these colonies were emerging as significant competitors in the export

OPPOSITE
The war's most famous general was Andrew Jackson. He later became US president, as did other veterans Willam Henry Harrison, John Tyler, Zachary Taylor, and James Buchanan. (Oil, c.1819, Metropolitan Museum of Art)

EASTERN NORTH AMERICA JUNE 1812

RUPERT'S LAND

LOWER CANADA

St Lawrence

NEWFOUNDLAND

St John's

Lake Superior

INDIANA TERR.

UPPER CANADA

Ottawa

Quebec

NEW BRUNSWICK

PEI

ILLINOIS TERRITORY

Mackinac

MICHIGAN TERRITORY

Lake Huron

Lake Michigan

York

Lake Ontario

Montreal

VT

MASS (Maine)

Halifax

NOVA SCOTIA

NH

Detroit

Lake Erie

Buffalo

NEW YORK

MASS

Boston

MISSOURI TERRITORY

INDIANA TERR.

OHIO

PENNSYLVANIA

CT RI

St Louis

Mississippi

NJ

New York

Philadelphia

DEL

Baltimore

Washington

MD

VIRGINIA

KENTUCKY

ATLANTIC OCEAN

TENNESSEE

NORTH CAROLINA

SOUTH CAROLINA

MISSISSIPPI TERRITORY

GEORGIA

Charleston

Savannah

Bermuda

WEST FLORIDA

New Orleans

LOUISIANA

EAST FLORIDA

GULF OF MEXICO

BAHAMAS

N

CUBA

British territory

United States

Spanish territory

Disputed territory between the US and Spain

0   250 miles

0   500 km

of North American products. Additionally, annexation would benefit US expansion elsewhere: in the west against Indigenous tribes by depriving them of help from British officials and Canadian fur traders; and in the south, where expansionists hoped that the subjugation of Canada would increase support for their goal of taking East and West Florida from Spain, then a British ally.

All these issues, along with a political crisis that threatened Madison's hold on power, led the United States to choose war over diplomacy in June 1812. A month later, American soldiers invaded Canada, heralding the beginning of three years of fighting that would plague the United States, Great Britain, its colonies, and many of the First Nations of eastern North America. In the following pages we will explore the story of the war on land and sea, study its causes and outcomes, and examine some of the conflict's important secondary themes.

***

This book is a thoroughly revised and enlarged version of one that Osprey published in 2002. As the author of the original, I am pleased to share this edition with readers, especially because it provides a late-career opportunity to summarize my thoughts on the war for general audiences. Aside from correcting a small number of errors, it benefits from the impressive advances in scholarship that have occurred over the last two decades. Beyond wide-ranging analytical reinterpretations, expanded archival research since 2002 has changed even basic assumptions, such as the dates when some battles occurred and the size of the opposing forces (although other details remain unclear or subject to debate). In addition, historians have examined subjects that had not received much attention before, or have re-evaluated long-standing themes of importance. Established authors, including the Canadian Donald Graves and the American Donald Hickey, have continued to add to our understanding, while new scholars, such as Americans Nicole Eustace and Adam Jortner, have emerged to make their contributions to the war's historiography. Across the Atlantic, British

The historic port of Quebec and capital of British North America was the strongest military position in Upper and Lower Canada. (Print, 1813, Library of Congress)

historians have devoted more attention to the events of 1812–15 than was common in the past, as represented by the work of Andrew Lambert. (In my own case, I have written two additional books and several articles on the subject since 2002 to add to my earlier efforts.) This edition also presents more images than the earlier one did, and most are different from those that appeared in the original. It is, therefore, my hope that readers will find this concise overview of one of North America's formative events to be both informative and enjoyable.

BACKGROUND TO WAR

A small war with complex causes

Sailors' rights

The *Chesapeake* affair symbolized how grave the issue of 'impressment' was between Great Britain and the United States. The number of seamen per ton of ship in the Royal Navy (RN) was worse than it was among other major maritime powers, and in its desperation to fill ships' companies in the war with France, it impressed men. This was a rough form of conscription, regarded as little more than legalized kidnappings in port towns and from merchant vessels by its victims and their families. Naturally, many impressed men deserted, as did others who had volunteered for the navy but who subsequently regretted their decision. Large numbers of them fled to foreign ships for asylum and employment, including to those of the United States. At the same time, foreign seamen – including Americans – who found themselves unemployed in ports far from home, joined the Royal Navy. They also often deserted. Legally, all of these individuals were liable to being returned to the navy, while Britons who had emigrated to the United States had statutory obligations to serve if impressed. Consequently, the RN stopped merchant ships to remove eligible men, but some officers illegitimately took citizens from other countries, including Americans, who neither had served in the British navy nor had links to King George III's dominions.

The number of sailors removed from American ships is uncertain, as is their citizenship, but the US government issued a report stating that 6,057 men had been seized from the republic's vessels between 1803 and 1811. The list was full of duplications and did not identify either British-born seamen or Americans who had deserted from the RN, although the document, due to poor reporting, also did not include others who had been taken illegally. Furthermore, a number of American officials undermined the credibility of their country's claims of injustice by selling false citizenship documents to sailors, as happened in London where a diplomat, for a small fee, sold such certificates to people who wanted them. Conversely, the British released illegally impressed people when their cases came to the attention of the authorities. Hence, the issue was more complex than commonly believed. Despite these ambiguities, impressment represented an affront to national sovereignty, and there can be no doubt that substantial

In 1811, the USS *President* engaged HMS *Little Belt* off Chesapeake Bay, inflicting heavy casualties on the smaller vessel. (Print, c.1811–12, photo by Print Collector/ Getty Images)

numbers of Americans were forced wrongfully into the Royal Navy.

When the *Leopard* fired on the *Chesapeake*, existing tensions between the two countries over impressment disintegrated into a crisis. Many Americans demanded a military response, believing that it was one thing to take people from merchant vessels, but something entirely different to attack a sovereign nation's warships. The British government, desperate to avert hostilities, repudiated the *Leopard*'s action, punished the officers responsible, offered compensation, and returned the three Americans. Likewise, the US president at the time, Thomas Jefferson, hoped to maintain peace, so the crisis passed. Nevertheless, anger and outrage continued to mark Anglo-American relations because impressment from merchant vessels did not stop.

Meanwhile, the United States Navy (USN) protected the country's neutrality whenever it could, and occasionally did so with an unnecessary degree of violence, as occurred in 1811 when the frigate USS *President* fired upon the RN sloop *Little Belt*, which its captain had mistaken for a different warship that had impressed some Americans. The smaller vessel lost 32 killed and wounded to only one person injured on the *President*. The government in Washington apologized but exonerated the frigate's captain. The British did not pursue the matter because they needed to focus their attention against Napoleon Bonaparte's aspirations to turn their island kingdom into a French vassal state; therefore, avoiding war with America was desirable because of the desperate European situation at the time.

Free trade

In addition to 'sailors' rights', problems surrounding the issue of 'free trade' contributed to the American decision to go to war. As a neutral nation, the United States faced serious challenges in gaining and expanding access to the world's markets while France and Britain fought each other. Despite this, US international trade grew immensely before 1812, largely through opportunities created by that very conflict. Then, around 1805–07, America's trade challenges intensified. Until that time, there had been enough problems: the United States had suffered from existing British and French restrictions, had seen hundreds of ships seized by both European powers, had engaged in combat against the French in the Quasi-War of 1797–1801 (mainly in the Caribbean Sea), and in a separate conflict had fought North African Barbary pirates between 1801 and 1805. Nevertheless, Britain regularly had ignored American ships that had violated a British policy that denied neutral vessels the right to replace those of belligerent powers in carrying goods between a combatant's ports, so long as American vessels 'broke' voyages by stopping in the US, thereby turning their cargoes into 'American' exports. In 1805, however, a British court decided that American shipowners ought to provide better evidence that they had fulfilled this obligation than they had been doing, although the government in London still decided not to enforce the decision. Nevertheless, in 1806 the king's ministers used orders-in-council to expand trade restrictions with its enemy. The orders (essentially being cabinet decisions) authorized a blockade of French-controlled ports (which the RN only partially enforced) and the apprehension of neutral ships unless they put into British ports to pay duties on their cargoes. The objective was not so much to cut commerce with France as to levy a tribute on merchants who traded with it and the countries it controlled. In fact, Crown officials granted thousands of licences every year to shipowners – including Americans – to trade with France. In that same year, Napoleon issued the first of several decrees to implement policies that he hoped would undermine the British economy by banning its imports, putting the United Kingdom under an almost-fictional blockade, and seizing merchant vessels, including those of the United States, that carried goods from Britain or its colonies, or that complied with British laws, or that violated French – and even American – trade regulations.

In theory, both countries' policies angered Americans equally, but Britain had the naval might to implement them more effectively, and thereby became the greater focus of outrage. The US government rejected the authority of the French and British restrictions, arguing that blockades only could be lawful if fully enforced, which neither power could do. The Americans, however, did not want war at that time, so they passed laws to limit or close trade with these (and other) countries between 1806 and 1811. The administration in Washington thought the European belligerents not only needed North American products to fight their wars, supply their manufacturers, and feed their people at home and in their colonies, but that they depended upon US ships to move these goods – as well as European and colonial products – across the world's oceans. (The American merchant fleet was the second largest on the planet after that of the British Empire.) By restricting or denying access to these goods and services, the government hoped to force France and Britain to make concessions, including opening more of the world's markets. The most famous of these laws was the Embargo Act of 1807. Fundamentally, it forbade American ships and

Britain's 1805 victory at Trafalgar strengthened its maritime dominance over Napoleon but undermined American interests, contributing to the 1812 US declaration of war. (Oil, 1808–24, photo © Christie's Images/ Bridgeman Images)

New York's Castle Williams of 1811 was one of a number of new defences designed to protect US Atlantic ports as Anglo-American relations deteriorated. (Print, 1824, Metropolitan Museum of Art)

goods from leaving the United States. However, it did not change London's views. Instead, it depressed the American economy and generated widespread opposition among the nation's residents. Many people in the republic evaded its restrictions by arranging clandestine shipments from their own shores or by smuggling goods though the British colonies on the country's northern border for transfer across the Atlantic Ocean.

In 1809, during the final days of the Jefferson administration, the United States replaced the Embargo with milder restrictions. It reopened trade with most countries but prohibited trade with France and Britain while offering to resume relations with whichever power changed its hurtful policies. This legislation likewise was ineffective, and in 1810, the government, now led by James Madison, re-established trade with everyone but allowed the president to impose non-importation on one of the European belligerents if the other repealed its restrictions. Without any serious ability to blockade Britain, Napoleon offered to suspend his decrees if the United Kingdom cancelled its orders-in-council or if the

United States imposed non-importation on Britain. Yet, he also issued a new decree that led the French to seize more American vessels in 1810 than the Royal Navy did. The normally astute but Anglophobic Madison either fell for the French ruse or chose to disregard Bonaparte's mendacious behaviour in order to advance American interests. In March 1811, the president imposed non-importation on Britain. This delighted the French emperor, who hoped that an Anglo-American war would follow and relieve some of the pressure the British exerted against his forces in Europe.

Expansionism

The British did not think they could comply with all of the American demands on trade or impressment, in part because the Royal Navy was their best weapon in the struggle against France, and so it had to be used as effectively as possible. Furthermore, the impact of American restrictions, although injurious, was not sufficient to force significant concessions, and the British were strong enough that they could look beyond the wartime crisis to the possibility that coercive measures might translate into an expansion of their own maritime economy at the expense of their competitors once peace returned. Moreover, when faced with the embargo and similar actions, they found alternative sources of supply. Naturally, their North American colonies promised to meet some of the Empire's needs. Through preferential trade and other measures, London fostered that potential at a time when the British North American provinces had developed to the point where they could produce valuable surpluses (stimulated partly by the vacuum created by Washington's trade restrictions). Between 1807 and 1811, for instance, their exports of softwood timber rose by 556 per cent. To strengthen the colonies further at the expense of the United States, the British government issued an order-in-council in 1811 that excluded American salted fish from the West Indian colonies and imposed heavy duties on other US imports.

This was a blow to President Madison. He had assumed that the Caribbean islands could not be fed without American fish. Thus, the British decision exposed the weakness of his trade policies as vehicles of coercion. It also underscored the extent to which the North American colonies had become rivals, both in their own

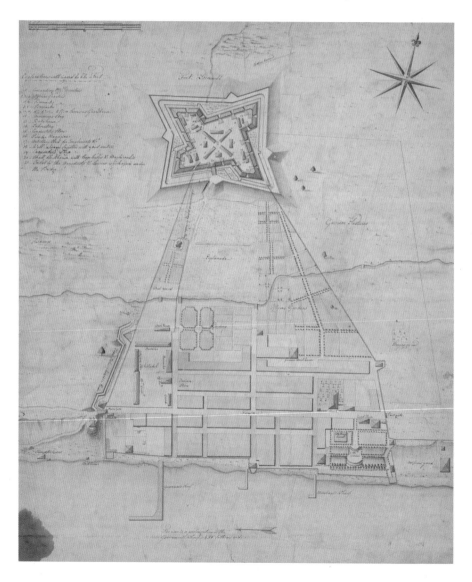

right and as conduits for smugglers within the United States to use in circumventing his restrictions. Looking to the future, Madison worried that the Great Lakes–St Lawrence waterway, part of which lay entirely within British territory, might evolve into the main route that Americans in the northern interior would use to ship their goods to Europe. The president therefore thought that conquering the British possessions would deny the United Kingdom (and other European powers) access to North American products except under conditions favourable to US interests – to say nothing of the impact annexation would have on the overall size, prosperity, and power of his nation.

Many Americans supported expansion because they thought expelling Britain from the continent represented a natural step in the republic's evolution. Congressman John Harper expressed this idea in 1812 when he proclaimed that no less an authority than 'the Author of Nature' had 'marked our limits in the south by the Gulf of Mexico; and in the north by the regions of eternal frost.' For others, seizing Canada would serve as a fitting punishment to avenge the country's problems on the high seas. Some expansionists wanted to profit personally from changing America's borders. Such were the aims of the entrepreneur and politician Peter B. Porter of Buffalo (who would command a brigade during the 1814 invasion of Canada). His views differed from Madison's because he thought both Upper and Lower Canada should be conquered but only the upper province should be absorbed into the American republic, while the lower, overwhelmingly francophone colony should be turned into an independent state. This vision fitted his business interests. He owned a carrying trade around Niagara Falls on the New York side of the border and assumed that the conquest of Upper Canada would allow him to put his competitors on the British side of the river out of business. Furthermore, he did not want inland commerce to move down the St Lawrence through the lower province because he promoted a canal system – the future Erie Canal – to move goods from the Great

OPPOSITE
Detroit's Fort Lernoult was typical of the poorly maintained and understrength pre-war forts garrisoned by both sides on the Canadian frontier. (Manuscript, 1799, William L. Clements Library, University of Michigan)

Lakes to the Hudson River and on to New York City. Having Lower Canada become a separate country would discourage the development of the St Lawrence route in order to keep America's transportation systems within the United States, as well as constrain its entrepreneurs from competing against his interests because of their status as foreigners.

Frontiers and borderlands

As debates over impressment, trade, and the destiny of British North America took place, other long-standing troubles on the republic's western and southern frontiers helped to persuade the United States to declare war. After the American Revolution of 1775–83, the First Nations of the 'Old Northwest' (in modern Ohio, Indiana, Illinois, Michigan, Wisconsin, and part of Minnesota) saw hundreds of thousands of hostile settlers take away their land and change the environment by cutting down forests, chasing away game, and thereby rendering existing subsistence economies incapable of meeting Indigenous needs. The Shawnees, Delawares, Wyandots, Potawatomis, Odawas, and others responded to these challenges by forming a confederacy in the latter 1780s to fight for their homelands. At the battle of the Wabash in 1791, they inflicted the greatest defeat the US ever endured at the hands of Indigenous peoples. In 1794, however, the tribes lost the battle of Fallen Timbers, and in 1795, surrendered much of the land that makes up today's Ohio, along with smaller tracts elsewhere, in return for a new boundary between themselves and the settlers. While their confederacy collapsed, the First Nations nonetheless hoped that the new border would allow their societies to evolve at their own speed and on their own terms in their remaining territories, but the lines drawn in 1795 proved to be only temporary. Immediately after their creation, American authorities continued to acquire land through aggressive – and often fraudulent – tactics, which drove Indigenous people farther west and north. In their desperation, they again thought of uniting to defend their remaining territories. In 1805, the Shawnee brothers Tenskwatawa and Tecumseh founded a new political and spiritual coalition, known to historians as the Western Tribes. Not everyone joined, including many who nevertheless would fight against the United States in the War of 1812. Furthermore, others would embrace neutrality and a small number would ally with the Americans.

The British were implicated in the frontier crisis in the pre-war years because they supplied weapons and other assistance to their old Revolutionary War allies during the frontier crisis of 1786–95 and then afterwards, especially as the possibility of a new Anglo-American conflict grew following the *Chesapeake* affair. In the struggles of the latter 1780s and early 1790s, Crown officials had

The Shawnee prophet Tenskwatawa (depicted), and his brother, the political and military leader Tecumseh, worked to unite Indigenous peoples against the United States. (Oil, c.1830–33, National Portrait Gallery, Smithsonian Institution, CC0)

The Shawnees (represented on the left) and Kaskaskias (right) formed part of the Western Tribes with Odawas, Ojibwas (Anishinabek), Kickapoos, Potawatomis, and others. (Prints 1805/26, Courtesy of the John Carter Brown Library, CC BY-SA 4.0)

hoped that Indigenous successes would allow them to help the tribes negotiate the creation of an independent homeland on Upper Canada's south-western border, which, aside from its benefits to the tribes, would have made the colony more defensible. At the same time, Canadian fur traders had moved freely through the region and had helped maintain the British alliance, to the fury of the Americans. Later, as new threats of war grew in the years immediately before 1812, the British continued to cultivate their alliance relationship with Indigenous peoples because they recognized that they needed First Nations support to protect Canada. Yet they also tried to defuse frontier tensions in hopes of avoiding hostilities with the United States altogether. Their activities naturally offended Americans, many of whom were convinced that the British were plotting against them, although their leaders generally recognized that the Crown's policies primarily were defensive. Anger within the republic grew when warriors from the Western Tribes attacked an American force at Tippecanoe in

November 1811 in which the white soldiers repelled their enemies and then burned the nearby community of Prophetstown, which had served as a capital for Tecumseh and Tenskwatawa's movement. Coming seven months before the beginning of the Anglo-American war, the battle heralded the beginning of increased violence between settler and Indigenous populations. The frontier crisis quickly amplified existing cries for the conquest of Canada in order to isolate the tribes from foreign aid and thereby ensure that their opposition to American expansion could be suppressed more easily.

Far to the south, expansionists thought that war against the First Nations and the conquest of Canada would help them achieve their own regional territorial ambitions. One of these areas comprised the extensive lands of the Muscogee (or Creek) confederation, largely within the Mississippi Territory, where tensions were similar to those in the Old Northwest. Additionally, the Americans wanted to annex the Spanish colonies of East and West Florida. As it was, they occupied part of West Florida before the outbreak of the War of 1812, but assumed that hostilities with Spain's ally, Britain, would facilitate their designs on the remainder of these territories.

Madison's political problems

Another factor that influenced James Madison's decision to go to war was his fear that he might lose the presidency in the election scheduled for late 1812. His perceived weakness in managing the nation's foreign affairs (along with additional issues) generated criticism and dissent within his own Democratic-Republican party, as well as from its Federalist opponents who wanted to negotiate better relations with Great Britain. Among other responses, the president felt compelled to take a strong stand against the British in order to regain the confidence of both his party and the nation's voters. Accordingly, he assumed he either had to achieve a settlement with London on American terms or go to war.

The negotiations that did take place were unsuccessful. The British argued that revoking the orders-in-council was wrong because Napoleon's actions were fraudulent; therefore, the US decision to invoke non-importation against the British made no sense, and in fact invited retaliation. Faced with factionalism among the Democratic-Republicans, Madison would not admit to having made a mistake in accepting Bonaparte's offer because that would have confirmed his adversaries' claim that he was incompetent. Consequently, the nation's interests and those of his own ambitions may have come into conflict. Realizing that many of his supporters opposed the government's ineffective trade policies at the same time that he developed his annexationist views towards British North America, Madison called Congress into session for November 1811 to prepare for war. His objectives were to secure the presidency in the coming election and increase the pressure on the British to relent. If the king's government did not, he intended to provide the country with the resources it needed to fight. In the end, Madison failed to improve the nation's military capabilities adequately and embarked on a dubious war but won re-election with 50.4 per cent of the vote.

The American rallying cry of 'free trade and sailors' rights', which ostensibly articulated the official reasons for war, was not the simple demand for justice presented in popular histories. It was fraught with its own ambiguities and, importantly, was compromised morally by expansionist desires directed against the First Nations, the Spanish colonies, and British North America. Hence, the War of 1812 had complex origins. It was a small war when compared with the great conflict in Europe. When it ended in 1815, for instance, the British and American militaries respectively had suffered 9,000 and 12,000 deaths due to combat, disease, and other causes (while Indigenous forces had endured an unknown but smaller number of fatalities). In contrast, the British army that struggled through the Peninsular War in south-western Europe between 1807 and 1814 experienced

60,000 deaths while the French lost between 180,000 and 240,000 men to British, Portuguese, and Spanish forces. Despite its relatively small size – but enormous geographical reach – the War of 1812 was important in the histories of the United States, Canada, the British Empire, and the First Nations.

WARRING SIDES
Soldiers, sailors, and warriors

Mistaken beliefs

For a country contemplating war against the world's greatest naval power while already engaged in hostilities against the tribes on its western frontiers, the United States did not prepare its military well. In part, Americans were confident in their regional superiority in North America to think that they did not need to invest heavily in the army and navy, especially because they did not expect Britain to reinforce its colonies adequately due to the war in Europe. Furthermore, many Americans distrusted standing military forces, believing that they might threaten their liberties. They also possessed an unreasonable faith in the country's militia, consisting of civilians with limited training, equipment, and essential administrative systems. President Madison was typical in his discomfort with a professional army and his embrace of the militia. He realized his mistake in 1814 when he saw the surprisingly fast defeat of a force comprised mainly of militia at the hands of smaller numbers of British regular soldiers at Bladensburg near Washington, remarking, 'I could never have believed that so great a difference existed between regular troops and a militia force, if I had not witnessed the scenes of this day.'

Naval forces

The United States Navy entered the conflict in better condition than the American army. With 7,250 sailors and marines in 1812, it enjoyed the leadership of competent officers and the skill of trained seamen, many of whom had seen action against the French navy and the Barbary pirates. Yet it had been undermined by inadequate funding and muddled political thinking in the pre-war years, and so was not as strong as it could have been. At the outbreak, the saltwater fleet had 13 operational vessels. Three of them were its famous heavy frigates *United States*, *Constitution*, and *President*; three were smaller frigates similar in size to those in the Royal Navy; and, in descending order, there were five sloops and two brigs. There were also 165 coastal gunboats, 62 of which were in commission. Of the vessels in reserve, the Americans repaired two frigates and converted one into a corvette during the war. They also built other vessels and integrated some captured British ships into their fleet.

In contrast, the Royal Navy was the world's most powerful maritime force following Vice-Admiral Horatio Nelson's victory over the combined French and Spanish fleets at Trafalgar in 1805. However, its size and successes masked serious problems. Notably, France continued to pose a grave threat at sea, which would prevent the RN from deploying significant resources to the western Atlantic unless the European situation improved, which the Americans did not expect to occur until they had conquered Canada, if

This American militia artillery coat is typical of the period's uniforms, which stylistically were similar to those of European armies. (Artefact, c.1812, © Don Troiani. All Rights Reserved 2023 / Bridgeman Images)

In 1812–15, the USS *Constitution* typically carried 30 24-pounders (depicted), and 22 carronades and other artillery pieces. It is now a ship museum in Boston. (Brian Jannsen / Alamy Stock Photo)

indeed it happened at all. For instance, Napoleon only had 34 ships-of-the-line (or main battleships) in 1807, having lost 30 in 1805–06, but he increased that number to 80 by 1813 with another 35 under construction. Meanwhile, Britain's ability to maintain equivalent vessels dropped from 113 to 98 between 1807 and 1814 as years of war with France strained the resources of the island kingdom's 12 million people. In addition, the Royal Navy's global commitments forced it to send under-strength, ill-trained, and partially impressed crews to sea, often in substandard vessels. Yet the sheer weight of the fleet promised to give the RN dominance over the USN if the European situation unfolded in favour of the United Kingdom.

Both sides expanded their freshwater capabilities on the Great Lakes and Lake Champlain. These were important initiatives because the undeveloped state of the region meant that water communications were essential for moving troops and supplies through the borderlands between the opposing powers. The British entered the conflict with the advantage of the Provincial Marine, a transport service for the army, which maintained two small ships and two schooners to serve Lake Ontario and the St Lawrence River as far east as Prescott (where the rapids shut off direct access to the rest of the river and the Atlantic beyond). To the west, on the other side of the great barrier at Niagara Falls, it operated four vessels on Lake Erie, one of which had a draught that was shallow enough to travel between Lake Erie and the upper lakes. On Lake Champlain, however, a single derelict schooner protected the king's interests. The Americans maintained two gunboats on Lake Champlain, but only one brig on

British spy C.H. Smith visited the United States in 1816–17, and then created this record of US Marine uniforms of the War of 1812. (Watercolour, 1816–45, HEW 15.8.5, Houghton Library, Harvard University)

United States Corps
of Marines.

each of Lakes Ontario and Erie. During the conflict, the two sides augmented their freshwater forces by taking merchant schooners into naval service, capturing enemy craft, and building new vessels at such a rapid pace that historians sometimes describe the contest for control of the Great Lakes as 'the shipbuilders' war'. For example, by August 1813, the British had increased their strength on Lake Ontario to six vessels carrying 97 guns and carronades, while the American squadron boasted 13 ships and schooners mounting 112 artillery pieces. The United States Navy possessed an advantage on the Great Lakes because its supply lines were much shorter, and because it could draw upon the far greater resources of its population and advanced economy in comparison to that of British North America. Furthermore, its war with Great Britain was its only Euro-American conflict, unlike that of the Royal Navy (which assumed command over the Provincial Marine's vessels in 1813).

The artillery used by the two navies usually consisted of guns – the 'cannon' of popular imagination – and carronades. The latter were short versions of guns that fitted well into the confined spaces of warships. Both fired on trajectories of between zero and five degrees, and both used the same ammunition. The main projectile was round shot – the famous 'cannonball'. It was a solid iron ball that smashed into and through its target but did not explode. Balls weighed 6, 9, 12, 18, 24 or 32 pounds (2.7, 4.1, 5.4, 8.2, 10.9 and 14.5 kilogrammes). The range of artillery pieces varied, with lighter guns firing shorter distances than heavier pieces. The maximum effective range of a common 6-pounder's round shot, for instance, was 1,200 yards (1,100m) and a 24-pounder's was 2,000 yards (1,800m). Carronades had shorter ranges; for example, that of a 24-pounder was 1,100 yards (1,000m). Among a selection of other munitions used, grape and canister shot were important as anti-personnel projectiles. They consisted of bags or tins full of small balls. When fired, the balls sprayed out in an arc to kill and maim enemy combatants, although they had shorter ranges than round shot, with 300 yards (275m) being typical. There were other forms of munitions used, but on a less-frequent basis. Gunners could use chain shot, consisting of two balls or two half-balls joined by a chain, to fire against the masts and rigging on ships. Another projectile was bar shot – an iron bar that often had a half cannon ball at each end – which was also effective against the upper sections of sailing vessels. Shore batteries firing against ships used the same projectiles but they also might heat round shot to create 'hot shot' that not only would break through a vessel's hull, but would set it on fire. While artillery were the primary weapons on warships, seamen used muskets, pistols, pikes, and cutlasses at close quarters.

Land forces

The land forces of the British and Americans were similar in terms of organization, weapons, and tactical doctrine, although the United States Army regularly enjoyed a numerical advantage while the king's soldiers normally benefited from stronger leadership and better training until the last year of the war, by which time their opponents had improved the competence of their regular forces. Like all Western armies, both had a mix of line and light infantry, as well as artillery, cavalry, engineers, and others. Both also relied on the services of part-time militiamen drawn from the civilian population. Indeed, the Americans called out over 450,000 militia during the war, a number equivalent to 90 per cent of the entire population of British North America. Additionally, both sides deployed soldiers whose competence fell between the professionalism of the regulars and the limitations of the militia, such as regiments of American volunteers and 'incorporated' Canadian militia.

The land war was primarily an infantry struggle, fought by men organized into regimental or battalion formations that varied in size, but commonly mustered 500–800 soldiers. For most, their principal firearm was the smoothbore, muzzle-loaded, single-shot,

flintlock musket. Using paper cartridges containing a ball and powder (and occasionally extra buckshot, especially in American service), a soldier could load and fire his weapon two or three times per minute.

In action, the musket could be reasonably accurate at 50 yards (45m) and remained deadly up to 150 (140m). After that, its potency declined rapidly. Until improvements in weapons technology occurred later in the 1800s, the most effective way of using muskets was to stand troops in tightly packed lines and fire massed volleys into the enemy at close range. In simplified terms, these volleys ideally would shatter the opposing line so that the winning side could use its secondary weapon, the bayonet, to drive its adversaries from the field if they had not already left. There were some adaptations to the rough North American environment, such as thinning the lines compared to European practice on occasion, but the fundamental principle of volley fire dominated deployment and combat operations for both armies.

As effective as these dense formations of infantry were – and it was these soldiers who decided the big battles – they could not be used in all of the situations in which foot soldiers had to engage. Armies also needed light infantry when conditions called for skirmishing, ambushing, or guarding the line infantry's front, flanks, and rear. In battle, light infantry often deployed in a thin line or chain ahead of the main force until it was ready to fight. This allowed their small numbers to cover a wider frontage than the formation they protected. It meant, however, that they could not produce the heavy volume of fire of line troops, which was their fundamental weakness. Essentially, light infantry tried to preserve the main body from harassment by covering it so that it could approach the enemy in as fresh a state as possible. Additionally, they might try to weaken the enemy line before the arrival of their own line. In retreat, light infantry might deploy to hold off pursuing troops long enough for the main force to escape. In an advance, they might rush ahead to thwart enemy efforts to recover from a setback or to capture positions of tactical value, such as bridges or places that might serve as strongpoints.

OPPOSITE
The British 95th Regiment, represented by the kneeling rifleman, served in the war. The Americans also clothed some light troops in green uniforms. (Print, 1812–15, Peter Newark Pictures / Bridgeman Images)

Another of British spy C.H. Smith's images depicts American artillerists in late-war uniforms beside a light gun – probably a 6-pounder – on a mobile field carriage. (Watercolour, 1816–45, HEW 15.8.5, Houghton Library, Harvard University)

The majority of light troops carried muskets, but some used rifles. The main differences between these weapons were that the barrel interiors of rifles were not smooth but had spiral grooves cut into them and they held tighter-fitting bullets. This meant that rifles could be more accurate than muskets and were dangerous at 300 yards (275m). However, they took longer to load, fouled from gunpowder residue quickly, and suffered from other challenges. These limitations prevented them from becoming the dominant infantry weapon until technological advances solved these problems several decades after the War of 1812 had ended.

United States Artillery.

In the confusion of popular history, a common view is that British infantry fought in tightly packed lines and the Americans deployed in an individualistic manner and used cover because of their knowledge on the North American environment. The reality was that light infantry formed a larger percentage of the British than American regular forces in the war, and all armies in the Western tradition recognized the need for a balance of line and light troops. In terms of technology, drill, tactics, and other aspects of their militaries, there were many more similarities than differences between the British and American soldiers who faced each other across the fields and forests of the Great Lakes in the north, the Atlantic coast on the east, and the Gulf regions to the south.

The artillery used on land was similar to that employed at sea, with guns being the dominant weapon, but with carronades seeing limited service, such as in fortifications for close-quarters defence. Likewise, round shot and canister were the most commonly used projectiles. Armies, however, used mortars and howitzers more often than navies did. These weapons fired on high-angled trajectories and used shells, or exploding shot, as their primary projectile. A shell was a hollow ball filled with gunpowder and equipped with a fuse. The fuse could be adjusted so the shell would explode at a predetermined number of seconds after being fired. The British – but not the Americans – also used spherical case shot, or shrapnel. It was a shell containing musket balls and a powder charge, which, when fired from howitzers, served as a kind of long-range canister shot by exploding over the heads of enemies to rain both shell fragments and balls down upon them. Both sides used rockets, although the British employed them much more frequently than their opponents did. Used on land and at sea, rockets fired artillery projectiles from a pole, obviating the need for heavy guns or howitzers, which made them far more portable. They were, however, less accurate, but were not as unreliable as some writers have imagined them to have been.

Indigenous forces

The populations of the First Nations were too small, and the lives of their people were too valuable to allow for high casualties of the kind Western armies experienced. The total warrior population across the Great Lakes and Old Northwest, for instance, was about 12,000 men, and most of them had non-military obligations to their families' well-being. Therefore, a fundamental principle of Indigenous warfare was to avoid losses, even to the point of abandoning objectives to preserve the lives of the men in a war party. In addition, the personal freedoms enjoyed by members of their societies, combined with their conceptualizations of masculinity, meant that someone's involvement in hostilities was more individualistic than in Euro-American armies. It depended upon a man's assessment of the opportunities to win glory as well as his sensitivity to omens and signs that might lead him to withdraw from a campaign. These factors contributed to a style of combat distinct from British and American modes of fighting, but which possessed broad similarities to that of light infantry combat in terms of how they deployed under fire.

The main weapons carried by warriors were muskets, rifles, tomahawks, and knives, although spears, swords, and pistols were not uncommon, and traditional clubs and bows saw limited use. Indigenous men preferred to ambush their adversaries or utilize tactics that mimicked ambush in order to mask their movements to reduce casualties, strike from an advantage, upset their enemy's equilibrium, and thereby hamper their opponents' attempts to react effectively. Accordingly, they might conceal themselves near a road until an enemy had passed, then attack from both the flank and the rear, with the latter blocking the line of retreat in order to demoralize their adversaries and increase the warriors' chances of success, as occurred at Beaver Dams in 1813. Once engaged, they often used war cries to try to unnerve their opponents, and they might keep up pressure by advancing in relays to prevent their surprised

foes from establishing an effective position from which to respond to an attack. If their enemies broke, they gave chase in hopes of killing and capturing as many of them as possible. If warriors retreated, they tried to minimize losses, normally through a careful fighting withdrawal until they could reach safety.

Formidable as these combatants were, they were not without their weaknesses. The threat of heavy casualties could force warriors out of battle or stop them from engaging altogether. Moreover, their tactics tended to work better in offensive rather than defensive engagements. Beyond these issues, the First Nations took to the field not as pawns of Euro-Americans, but as allies with their own goals. Therefore, their participation alongside white forces on campaign was conditional. Often white commanders failed to recognize these basic facts when they wanted warriors to achieve an objective that did not meet Indigenous interests, and thus complained unfairly about the 'unreliability' of their First Nations allies. For the Americans, however, especially in 1813 and 1814, Indigenous men provided their most effective light troops on the northern front. For the British, warriors formed a markedly higher percentage of their total strength, making them especially significant because the numerical balance of the opposing sides normally favoured the Americans.

Pipe tomahawks were light tools and weapons that combined a small axe with a functional pipe. Euro-Americans made them to a 1740s Indigenous design concept. (Artefact, 1800–30, McCord Stewart Museum)

OUTBREAK
America sets its sights on Canada

The declaration of war

In November 1811, President James Madison asked Congress to prepare for hostilities. Much of the debate through the ensuing months was led by the 'War Hawks'. They mainly were younger men from frontier regions, such as Peter B. Porter, who saw the expansion of the republic's borders and the destruction of Indigenous resistance as fundamental objectives, and who demanded more aggressive approaches in dealing with Britain than had occurred in previous years. In contrast, politicians who represented the seaboard areas and shipping interests tended to oppose the slide towards belligerency. On 1 June 1812, Madison asked Congress to declare war, listing impressment, interference with trade, and British intrigue in the Old Northwest as causes, but remaining silent on the conquest of Canada and other matters. He was not concerned about articulating objectives or be completely truthful; his aim was to blame Great Britain and exonerate the United States for the need to fight. On 18 June, after favourable votes of 79 to 49 in the House of Representatives and 19 to 13 in the Senate, his country went to war.

In the final months of peace, the government in London had hoped to avert a conflict in which it would try to defend its North American colonies against heavy odds

while Britain's military forces could not reinforce them effectively because of the European war. Furthermore, American trade restrictions, while not meeting Madison's objectives, nonetheless had hurt commercial interests in the United Kingdom and had generated calls for relief from its manufacturers and merchants. The problem for the king's ministers rested on the concessions they could make. There was no reason to offer territory, and British officials did not believe their activities among the Great Lakes tribes were wrong because they were defensive in focus and because they worked to deter frontier tensions from escalating so long as the United States remained at peace with Britain. On the world's oceans, the Royal Navy's desperate manpower problems precluded relenting on impressment. In a major concession, however, the government of Prime Minister Lord Liverpool (Robert Jenkinson) revoked the offending orders-in-council on trade. It did so on 23 June 1812, not knowing that the Americans had decided to fight a week earlier. When word of this significant concession crossed the Atlantic, it was not enough to inspire President Madison to stop fighting and resume negotiations.

Fort George was one of the British border posts in Canada. It and its rival, Fort Niagara, sat within artillery range of each other. (Watercolour, 1805, William L. Clements Library, University of Michigan)

OPPOSITE
Worried about a
possible American
attack, Canadian
authorities ordered
US citizens to leave
Quebec City at the
outbreak of war in
order to improve
its security. (Poster,
1812, McCord
Stewart Museum,
Gift of the Misses
Fairchild)

The strategic situation

Americans confidently predicted that the conquest of Canada would occur quickly. In 1812, Thomas Jefferson claimed that 'the acquisition of Canada this year as far as the neighbourhood of Quebec, will be a mere matter of marching, and will give us experience for the attack on Halifax the next, and the final expulsion of England from the American continent.' The *National Intelligencer* expressed the Madison administration's view that the whole of Canada west of Quebec was 'in the power of the U. States because it consists of a long and slender chain of settlers unable to succour or protect each other and separated only by a narrow water from a populous and powerful part of the Union', and further argued that the fortified city of Quebec could be reduced through siege. All that was needed, according to the newspaper, was an army of 20,000, only one-third of which had to consist of regular forces.

There were good reasons for American confidence. British North America's population was 500,000 people, compared to 7.7 million in the United States, while the front-line province of Upper Canada only had 75,000 settlers. A large percentage of them were United Empire Loyalists who had moved there as refugees from the American Revolution or were their children, and who might be expected to stand firm. The majority, however, were recent immigrants from the republic who had been attracted to the colony because it was easier to acquire land there than on their own country's frontiers and who might welcome annexation. This concerned the British commander in Upper Canada, Major-General Isaac Brock, who thought it might be unwise to arm more than 4,000 of the 11,000 men of the province's militia. In Lower Canada, the majority of the population was French-Canadian, conquered by the British in 1763 during the Seven Years War, and which had shown only limited support for the Crown during the American Revolution. While French language and Roman Catholic rights were protected under British law,

POLICE.

WHEREAS authentic intelligence has been received that the Government of the United States of America did, on the 18th instant, declare War against the United Kingdom of Great Britain and Ireland and its dependencies, Notice is hereby given, that all Subjects or Citizens of the said United States, and all persons claiming American Citizenship, are ordered to quit the City of Quebec, on or before TWELVE o'clock at Noon, on WEDNESDAY next, and the District of Quebec on or before 12 o'clock at noon on FRIDAY next, on pain of arrest. ROSS CUTHBERT, C. Q. S. & Inspector of Police.

The Constables of the City of Quebec are ordered to assemble in the Police Office at 10 o'clock to-morrow morning, to receive instructions.

Quebec, 29th June, 1812.

officials doubted that these francophone subjects would rally with enthusiasm to repel an invasion.

The British also worried about the intentions of the Indigenous populations in the two Canadas. Unlike many people on the American frontier who opposed the United States, most of those who lived in the colonies were undecided about what to do. Some were willing to fight, but others assumed that the Americans would overwhelm the provinces and did not want to be punished for joining the losing side. Many were unhappy about how the Crown treated them over the alienation of land and the amount of independence they could exercise in the face of increasing settler intrusions into their lives, so they had reasons to be unresponsive when its officials approached them for assistance. The situation was uncertain enough that British commanders were afraid that a number of First Nations communities might join the Americans once an invasion occurred in order to buy peace with the United States in hopes of protecting their lands. Such an event would discourage militiamen from leaving their families unguarded when called away from their homes, and consequently might pose insurmountable challenges for the colony's military leaders.

Another reason American leaders expected to conquer the British provinces easily was that the garrison in the Canadas numbered only 6,000 soldiers in 1812 and could not be reinforced substantially while Napoleon menaced Britain. Furthermore, the bulk of these troops had to guard Montreal and Quebec. Montreal needed to be protected in order to keep the St Lawrence River open so that troops and supplies could be moved to the upper province; otherwise the colony would be doomed. If Montreal could not be held, the troops deployed around it had to be able to retreat to Quebec, the strongest position in British North America, in the expectation that a relief force, if available, could cross the Atlantic and rescue it before trying to recover enemy-occupied territory farther west. This strategy, logical as it was, meant that the upper province entered the war defended

by only 1,600 regulars. If the Americans were to gain control of the Great Lakes, however, Upper Canada probably would be lost unless it could be restored through diplomacy.

Yet the US Army was not as formidable as its opponents feared. In June 1812, its authorized strength was 35,600, but less than half that number had been enlisted, and a significant portion of them were untrained recruits. In addition, it had to garrison posts across the republic, so that only part of its strength could be deployed on the northern borders. Nevertheless, Upper Canada sat exposed to American seizure, and Lower Canada may have been in danger as well. It is difficult to imagine, however, that Jefferson's desire to conquer the Atlantic colonies could be achieved unless Britain faced a decisive defeat in Europe at the hands of Napoleon. As news of Napoleon's invasion of Russia crossed the Atlantic later in 1812, many people in the US thought Britain in fact would fall once Bonaparte crushed Tsar

Poor roads and seasonal restrictions created logistical challenges for armies. Water routes were best, but Niagara Falls, rapids, and other barriers impeded movement. (Print, 1798, Courtesy of the John Carter Brown Library, CC BY-SA 4.0)

Alexander I's forces and turned his huge armies against the United Kingdom. They even predicted that a French victory would be followed by a revolution that would overthrow the established order across the British Isles. That would not happen, and Napoleon's invasion of Russia degenerated into one of military history's great catastrophes.

Opening moves

Early in April 1812, the United States implemented an embargo on international trade so that its merchant ships could return home before hostilities began and thereby avoid falling into British hands. With the outbreak of war in mid-June, a squadron of five warships left New York with the objective of capturing a British merchant convoy heading to the United Kingdom from Jamaica, but it shifted its attention on 23 June when it sighted the Royal Navy frigate *Belvidera*. The frigate's captain, not being sure if war had begun, watched the squadron

These guns, protecting the Royal Navy's Nova Scotia base at Halifax, have been mounted on traversing carriages to maximize their field of fire. (Print, 1801, Library and Archives Canada)

carefully. As soon as the Americans opened fire, he ordered his ship north. The Americans pursued it, and both sides inflicted casualties, but the *Belvidera* escaped to Halifax, Nova Scotia to herald the outbreak of war. In the process, it saved the convoy by diverting the opposing naval vessels.

At about the same time, the crew of the American privateer *Dash* spotted a small RN schooner, the *Whiting*, lying at anchor in Hampton Roads on the American coast, and quickly overwhelmed its crew, who were unaware of Washington's declaration of war. As the *Whiting* had been sent to the United States to deliver diplomatic dispatches, the Madison administration released the vessel, but it did not make it back to England, being captured on the way by a French privateer, symbolizing how Britain now had to fight two distinct but overlapping wars. The Americans and French rarely cooperated against their common enemy, however. One exception occurred in 1814, when HMS *Majestic* beat off two French frigates, an American privateer, and other craft, and captured one of the enemy ships in the process.

On the northern front, the Americans ordered their armies to make a simultaneous multi-pronged invasion of Canada across the Detroit, Niagara, and St Lawrence rivers. The plan promised to divide the outnumbered defenders and by this means weaken them, and with the taking of Montreal, guarantee the fall of Upper Canada. However, the US Army, led predominantly by older political appointees who could not call upon adequate administrative and supply systems to meet their needs, failed to execute a coordinated offensive. Instead, the incursions came piecemeal over several months, the first occurring in July, when Brigadier-General William Hull led his troops across the Detroit River into Upper Canada.

THE FIGHTING
The war on land and sea

The Great Lakes–St Lawrence front

The primary theatres in the War of 1812 lay along the upper St Lawrence River and across the Great Lakes because the conquest of British territory was the primary military objective of the United States. America's other main territorial ambition – the elimination of Indigenous nations within the republic that blocked expansion – assumed that the fall of Canada would deprive them of the trade, diplomatic, and military support they needed to defend their interests. Therefore, American soldiers crossed into Canada in each of 1812, 1813, and 1814, intending to fulfil the government's expectations, and they won a number of important, even legendary, victories. Yet in only one of the eight invasion attempts did they occupy any British territory for more than a short and contested period; and that land, in south-western Upper Canada, was returned to Great Britain in the peace treaty.

The British countered the American desire to conquer their colonies by defending them as best they could, and through land and sea counter-offensives directed either from Canada or launched from ships against the Atlantic and Gulf coasts of the United States. The latter were designed to make the Americans redeploy military resources away from Canada, force an end to the conflict, and avenge the sufferings of the colonial population.

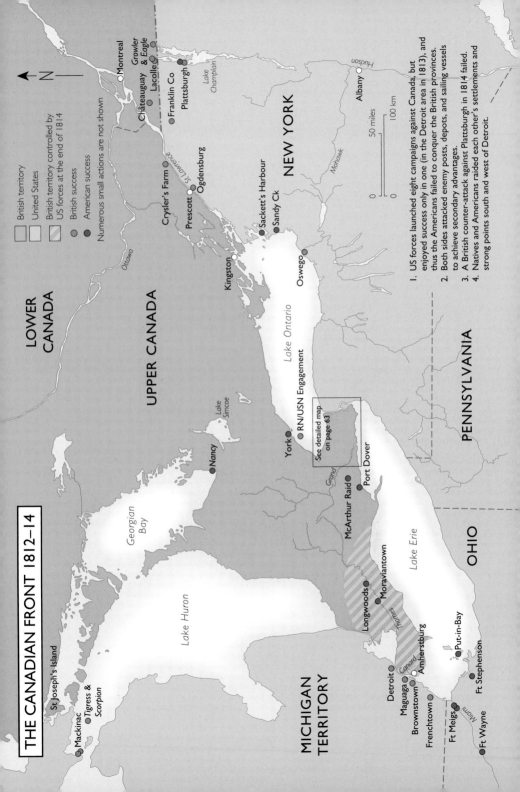

THE CANADIAN FRONT 1812–14

LOWER CANADA

UPPER CANADA

NEW YORK

PENNSYLVANIA

OHIO

MICHIGAN TERRITORY

Lake Huron

Georgian Bay

Lake Ontario

Lake Erie

Lake Champlain

Lake Simcoe

St Lawrence

Ottawa

Hudson

Mohawk

Grand

Thames

Canard

Miami

← N

British territory

United States

British territory controlled by
US forces at the end of 1814

British success

American success

Numerous small actions are not shown

0   50 miles
0   100 km

Montreal
Growler & Eagle
Châteauguay
Lacolle
Franklin Co
Plattsburgh
Albany
Ogdensburg
Crysler's Farm
Prescott
Sackett's Harbour
Sandy Ck
Kingston
Oswego
York
RN/USN Engagement
Nancy
See detailed map
on page 63
Port Dover
McArthur Raid
Longwoods
Moraviantown
Put-in-Bay
Amherstburg
Detroit
Maguaga
Brownstown
Frenchtown
Ft Meigs
Ft Stephenson
Ft Wayne
Mackinac
Tigress & Scorpion
St Joseph's Island

1. US forces launched eight campaigns against Canada, but
   enjoyed success only in one (in the Detroit area in 1813), and
   thus the Americans failed to conquer the British provinces.
2. Both sides attacked enemy posts, depots, and sailing vessels
   to achieve secondary advantages.
3. A British counter-attack against Plattsburgh in 1814 failed.
4. Natives and Americans raided each other's settlements and
   strong points south and west of Detroit.

If the British also managed to occupy some territory in the process, then they thought the international border might be redrawn to improve Canada's defensibility, especially if Indigenous homelands could be created in the Old Northwest. Nonetheless, their primary objectives were to retain their colonies and protect their maritime

Men from the fur-trade community and British army post at St Joseph's on Lake Huron, with Indigenous support, captured Fort Mackinac in July 1812. (Watercolour, 1804, William L. Clements Library, University of Michigan)

interests, and thus the war for Britain essentially was
a defensive one.

1812

When William Hull crossed the border into Upper
Canada in July 1812, General Brock decided to strike

back at the invaders with energy. He believed he had to demonstrate British strength in order to reassure the colony's settlers, as well as the First Nations whose help he needed if the province were to have any chance of survival. Fortunately for Brock, Hull's invasion faltered almost as soon as it began. Instead of marching on the British fort at Amherstburg to force his opponents out of the Detroit River region and intimidate the Indigenous and colonial populations into submission, a nervous Hull dithered, engaged in minor skirmishing, and worried that his army might be too weak to achieve its objectives. (Only one of his four regiments consisted of regulars; the others were militia.) One reason for Hull's caution lay in the fact that the British had captured a vessel on Lake Erie carrying his baggage, medical supplies, and important papers. That loss exacerbated his troubles, especially because his overland supply line ran largely through dismal swamplands threatened by Tecumseh's followers who had moved up to the Detroit region from the south-west at the outbreak of hostilities.

Meanwhile, far to the north, on Brock's orders, 50 soldiers from St Joseph's Island in Lake Huron, accompanied by several hundred fur traders and warriors, quietly surrounded the 61-man US garrison at Fort Mackinac on 17 July. The American commandant, facing a hopeless situation, surrendered. (The appearance of this hostile force was the first indication he received about the outbreak of war because his superiors did not send him a timely warning.) This bloodless victory was significant for the British: it secured their northern fur trade operations, allowed them to occupy the better-built US post instead of St Joseph's, helped to strengthen southward connections through Lake Michigan to the tribes of the upper Mississippi River, and inspired large numbers of Indigenous people across the upper lakes to take up arms against the United States.

When Hull learned about the fall of Mackinac, he assumed that the tribes along the Detroit border, hitherto neutral (unlike Tecumseh's followers), would rise against him and perhaps fall upon the settlers on the

American frontier. As he worried about the situation in the west, he learned that the campaign against Montreal, far to the east, designed in part to assist his efforts by dividing British forces, had been postponed. Closer to home, Hull received further frightening news when the Western Tribes attacked a supply column on its way to Detroit at Brownstown on 5 August and then beat off a force sent to oppose them. Consequently, he began withdrawing men from Canada on 7 August to secure his army inside Detroit. He also sent a plea for reinforcements so he could resume the offensive, and he ordered the garrison at Fort Dearborn (now Chicago) to withdraw in anticipation of widespread Indigenous hostilities. Hull dispatched 600 men south from Detroit to reopen communications, but British and First Nations forces ambushed them at Maguaga on 9 August. The Americans repulsed the attack but failed to achieve their objective and sustained heavy casualties. As they retired to Detroit, the Provincial Marine demonstrated its mastery on Lake Erie by subjecting them to a barrage along those sections of the road that ran past the shoreline. Now thoroughly demoralized, Hull withdrew his remaining troops from Canada on 11 August. Four days later, a Potawatomi force killed or captured the soldiers from Fort Dearborn as they tried to comply with Hull's orders to retire to Detroit.

Isaac Brock arrived on the Detroit River from Niagara on 13 August. Two days later, he demanded William Hull's surrender and tried to unnerve him by threatening massacre: 'It is far from my intention to join in a war of extermination,' he wrote, 'but you must be aware, that the numerous body of Indians who have attached themselves to my troops will be beyond control the moment the contest commences.' Hull retained sufficient nerve to reject the summons and was wise enough to realize that the threat probably was an empty one, but after a cross-river artillery bombardment on the night of 15–16 August, followed by a British advance against the settlement on the Michigan side of the border, his resolve collapsed. Before Brock's men could get within range of Detroit, Hull lowered the American flag over the town. To a mixed force of 1,400 regulars, militia, and warriors, Hull surrendered 2,200 men, impressive quantities of weapons and supplies, and the whole of the Michigan Territory. (During the war, prisoners often were 'paroled', enabling them to go home but not return to service until 'exchanged' with parolees from the opposing side. Others were kept in captivity in conditions that varied from the near-total freedom within the confines of a town that some officers enjoyed, to brutal close confinement in unhealthy conditions, especially for the lower ranks. People captured by warriors might be turned over to white allies in return for payment or be adopted into a First Nations community, where a few chose to remain, although small numbers of captives were tortured or murdered.)

The fall of Detroit was a critical victory for Brock. He had strengthened his western flank, acquired desperately needed equipment for his poorly armed militia, and sent a powerful signal to bolster the faithful, encourage the

Euro-Americans equipped Indigenous allies with various weapons, such as this British 'Indian contract pistol', similar in design to those used by cavalrymen. (Artefact, c.1814, © National Army Museum / Bridgeman Images)

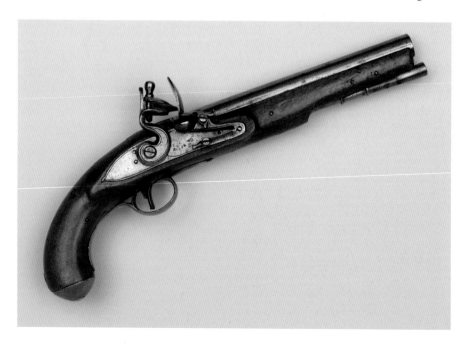

wavering, and subdue the disloyal in the settler and Indigenous populations of Upper Canada. Importantly, most of the Haudenosaunee (or Iroquois) of the Six Nations Tract along the Grand River north of Lake Erie joined the British in the aftermath of the fall of Detroit, adding 400 men to augment the small Upper Canadian garrison, while previously only a small percentage of the community's men had been willing to fight.

With the approach of autumn, the Americans mustered several thousand regulars, volunteers, and militia along the Niagara River for a second invasion of Upper Canada. They wanted to cut the province in two, seize superior winter quarters, demoralize the population, and wipe away the disgrace of Hull's debacle. However, they were badly trained, poorly equipped, and endured poor camp hygiene, all of which combined to undermine their effectiveness, demoralize the soldiers, and spread sickness. Additionally, tensions between the senior officers – Brigadier-General Alexander Smyth of the army and Major-General Stephen Van Rensselaer of the New York Militia – stopped them from working together. Consequently, when Van Rensselaer's men crossed the border, the majority of Smyth's troops remained in camp.

The thrust came on the night of 12–13 October 1812. Batteries along the length of the Niagara River opened fire on British positions while Van Rensselaer's troops rowed across the waterway between the villages of Lewiston and Queenston. As they got out into the current, they came under fire and suffered heavily. Nevertheless, they persevered, reached the Canadian shore, secured their landing, and found a way to the top of Queenston Heights – a natural ridge that dominated the village below and the surrounding countryside. General Brock counter-attacked up the steep heights in a frontal charge at the head of a comparatively small British and Canadian force. The Americans opened fire, Brock fell mortally wounded, and the charge quickly faltered.

Brock's successor, Major-General Roger Sheaffe, ordered more troops and warriors from posts along the river to converge on the American landing. At the same time, small detachments of British soldiers kept the invaders out of the village and continued to harass the boats ferrying men and supplies across the river. Of the reinforcements, a group of warriors – mainly Haudenosaunee – were the first to arrive. They ascended the heights inland, out of sight of the Americans, then

This impression of the 1812 battle of Queenston Heights shows three of its phases at once: the American landing, death of Isaac Brock, and US defeat. (Print, 1816, McCord Stewart Museum, Gift of David Ross McCord)

attacked from behind the cover of forest and scrub. Although vastly outnumbered, they kept their ill-trained enemy confined to relatively open and vulnerable ground close to the riverside cliff of the heights. One significant factor in their success was the absence of enough competent US light infantry to drive them away from the American line standing exposed in the open.

Hence, the soldiers fired heavy but ineffectual volleys at the Indigenous combatants in the brush to their front, while their opponents returned fire with fewer shots but with greater effect.

Haudenosaunee efforts enabled Sheaffe to assemble more warriors, regulars, militia, and volunteers on top of the heights out of range of his enemy. He then led them across flat ground against the Americans, whose morale and cohesion had been enfeebled by the warriors on the heights and the soldiers in the village below. Furthermore, the Americans, having expended much of their ammunition, felt trapped because their compatriots – frightened by the Indigenous presence and British fire – refused to row back across the river, either to reinforce or to rescue them. Sheaffe's men marched forward, fired one volley, and charged. Within 15 minutes it was over. Thus, the Americans experienced another humiliation and lost a large percentage of their force as casualties and prisoners. Within a week, hundreds of other dispirited men deserted from the military camps on the New York side of the Niagara River.

In November, Alexander Smyth led another American thrust across the Niagara River, near Fort Erie at Frenchman's Creek (or Red House) but cancelled the invasion when faced with strong British opposition. To the east, US forces made two half-hearted attempts against Montreal from Plattsburgh but withdrew when they encountered resistance from defending forces.

The outcome of the 1812 campaigns along the Canadian border was not the one most people on either site had expected. The Americans were defeated in every significant confrontation against the British and sustained huge losses in prestige, supplies, and men. They even lost enough territory to allow many in the Western Tribes to think that the dream of an independent Indigenous homeland might be achieved. Yet, the Americans enjoyed successes against the First Nations on the western borderlands when they repulsed attacks against Forts Harrison, Madison, and Wayne, and burned villages along the Mississinewa River and

OPPOSITE
The British usually were better equipped for Canadian winters than the Americans were in terms of clothing, snowshoes, and other necessities. (Print, 1812–15, © National Army Museum / Bridgeman Images)

elsewhere. These events, combined with the natural strength of the United States, suggested that Hull's great land surrender at Detroit might be overturned in a coming campaign.

1813

Both Great Britain and the United States strengthened their forces along the Canadian-American border over

INFANTRY OFFICER, in MARCHING ORDER.

the winter and spring of 1812–13 in anticipation of
the second season's campaigns. Despite their European
commitments, Lord Liverpool's government managed
to spare five additional infantry battalions, part of a
cavalry regiment, and other reinforcements for the
American war. Within the Canadian colonies, some
militiamen either formed incorporated battalions for
full-time service or joined smaller full-time units, such
as the Niagara Light Dragoons. The Royal Navy took
command of the Provincial Marine and added 470
officers and ratings to the crews of the freshwater ships
and brought along skilled tradesmen to build up the
Great Lakes squadrons. In the United States, Congress
authorized 20 new infantry regiments, approved an
expansion of the navy, and sent hundreds of seamen to
the Great Lakes from the Atlantic, where a developing
British blockade of the eastern seaboard prevented part
of the saltwater fleet from setting sail.

The first land battles of 1813 occurred in the Detroit
region. The Americans sent an army to regain the
territory that had been lost in 1812, but the British under
Colonel Henry Procter defeated its advanced guard in
the January snows at Frenchtown (now Monroe). To
the east, in February, the British captured Ogdensburg
in an effort to weaken the American threats to the St
Lawrence lifeline that connected Upper Canada to the
rest of the Empire.

Meanwhile, in Washington, Secretary of War John
Armstrong thought the first target in the upcoming
campaign should be Kingston and the naval squadron
anchored there. If the British lost their warships on
Lake Ontario, they most likely would not be able to
hold Upper Canada. The American army and navy
commanders on the northern front – Major-General
Henry Dearborn and Commodore Isaac Chauncey –
opposed attacking Kingston because they overestimated
the strength of its fortifications. Instead, they thought
that weakly defended York (now Toronto) should be
seized. They argued that the capture of two warships
believed to be in the town would swing the balance of

power on the lake to the United States and facilitate the second and third phases of their proposed plan – the capture of the Niagara Peninsula, followed by offensive operations against either Kingston or Montreal later in the year. At first, Washington rejected the scheme, realizing that Armstrong's strategy was better, but the Madison administration eventually accepted it for political reasons. The pro-war governor of New York, Daniel Tompkins, sought re-election in April 1813 but feared defeat through voter disenchantment with the lack of progress in the conflict. A victory on the Canadian front would encourage voters to choose Tompkins. York was a good target because of its vulnerability and because its capture would have good propaganda value since it was the capital of the province.

The Americans sailed from Sackett's Harbour at the south-east corner of Lake Ontario; then, on 27 April, they launched an amphibious assault against York. Outnumbering its defenders, they drove Major-General Sir Roger Sheaffe out of the capital and took or destroyed substantial quantities of supplies. They did not get the ships, however: one had left shortly before the attack,

Postdating the battle of York, these 1813 blockhouses boast bullet-proof timber walls under the weatherboarding, loopholes for firing at an enemy, basement magazines, and other defensive features. (Walker Bibikow/Getty Images)

and the British burned the other before retreating towards Kingston. Through delays brought on by bad weather, the battle took place too late to have a legitimate influence on the election. Nevertheless, Tompkins's supporters had circulated victory proclamations to an unsuspecting electorate before the assault occurred and Dearborn kept his New York troops in New York to vote for the governor, with the result that Tompkins won the election by a small margin. During the week-long occupation of York, the Americans burned the residence of the colony's governor and its parliament buildings in contravention of the surrender negotiated by the town's leading citizens.

After occupying York, the Americans returned to Sackett's Harbour before implementing the second phase of the Dearborn–Chauncey plan. On 25 May, the guns of Fort Niagara and the US Lake Ontario squadron began a two-day barrage of Fort George at the mouth of the Niagara River before landing troops near the now-destroyed fort. About 1,400 soldiers, militiamen, and warriors met the 4,700 Americans (who enjoyed additional support from the navy and the men stationed on the New York side of the river). The defenders could not repulse the attack, so they abandoned not only Fort George but, one day later, the rest of their posts along the Niagara River to retreat to Burlington Heights (now Hamilton). So far, the Dearborn–Chauncey plan seemed to be working as American troops occupied the former British posts and rebuilt Fort George to secure their Upper Canadian foothold. At that point, the province was on the brink of being cut in half, with British and Indigenous forces to the west of the Niagara River facing the possibility that their already poor supply lines might be severed completely. As it was, the retreat from one of the posts, Fort Erie, allowed the Americans to send two vessels – previously trapped near Buffalo by British artillery – west to join the squadron being built on Lake Erie to challenge the Royal Navy later in the year. In addition, an attempt by the British to destroy Sackett's Harbour on 29 May while the USN squadron was away at the western end of Lake Ontario failed, further demoralizing Upper Canada's defenders.

On the Niagara Peninsula, Henry Dearborn followed his success at Fort George by sending troops to expel the British from Burlington Heights and make them retreat to Kingston. He was motivated partly by intelligence that the Grand River Haudenosaunee worried that the Americans might make a punitive

OPPOSITE

American forces captured Fort George in May 1813; the British then blockaded them in the post and neighbouring town from June to October. (Manuscript detail, 1810, Library and Archives Canada)

attack against their settlements since there now was nothing to stop them from such a strike. Concerned to preserve their territory, many considered abandoning the British, and some even thought of buying American forgiveness by falling upon the redcoats if they retreated eastwards. Consequently, as Dearborn dispatched 3,000

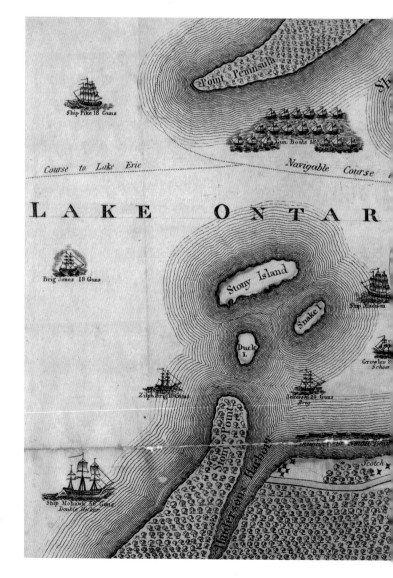

In 1813, the British unsuccessfully attacked Sackett's Harbour, the main American naval base on Lake Ontario. Note the fortifications and other military features. (Print, 1815, William L. Clements Library, University of Michigan)

infantry, artillery, and cavalry towards Burlington, warriors assembled near the British camp but, with the exception of a handful of them, refused to support the king's forces when asked to help. On 5 June, the Americans camped at Stoney Creek for the night to rest before the assault.

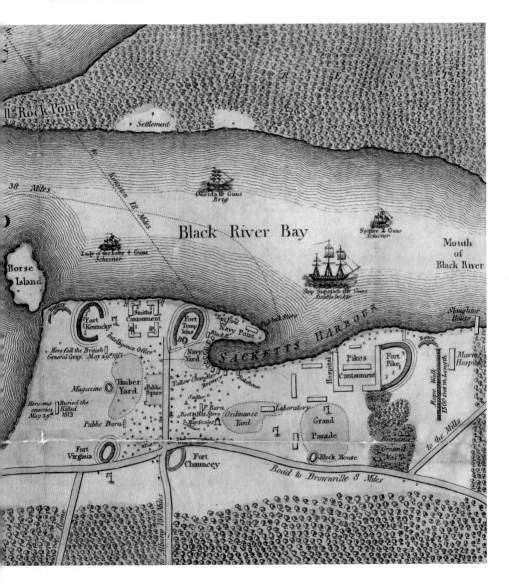

Recognizing the American and potential Indigenous threats, and agonizing over the fate of the Canadian population, the British made a desperate decision. Rather than await the Americans, they launched a surprise night attack against their enemy with 765 men early in the morning on 6 June. The ensuing battle of Stoney Creek was a violent and confused affair: friend shot at friend, and the two American brigadier-generals walked into the hands of British troops because they could not distinguish blue from red uniforms in the darkness. After sharp fighting, the British withdrew, but they had achieved their objective because the Americans cancelled their plans and retired to a camp on the Lake Ontario shoreline at Forty Mile Creek. The majority of the Grand River people cautiously decided to maintain their alliance with the British, which solidified further as events unfolded over the following days.

Shortly after the battle, a small group of warriors ambushed an American patrol and chased it into the newly established camp. At about the same time, the Royal Navy squadron, which had sailed west from Kingston to support the army, bombarded the site, and then captured 17 or 18 bateaux full of supplies. The Americans then abandoned much of their equipment and fled to Fort George by 9 June, with Canadian militia and warriors pursuing them to capture stragglers and supplies. Fearing a counter-offensive, General Dearborn evacuated all of the newly occupied positions along the Niagara River except Fort George. The British, led by Major-General John Vincent, reoccupied the vacant positions and prepared to blockade Fort George with the objective of preventing the Americans from posing a threat to the province beyond the post and neighbouring town of Niagara. Meanwhile, Indigenous reinforcements from the east, north, and west arrived, until Vincent had more than 800 warriors with him.

Dearborn responded to the developing challenge by organizing a secret expedition to destroy an important forward British position near Beaver Dams. About 600 infantry, cavalry, and artillery marched from Fort George south towards Queenston before swinging inland against

THE NIAGARA FRONT 1812–14

Upper Canada

New York

US territory controlled by British forces at the end of 1814

British success

American success

Numerous small actions are not shown

1. The British repulsed US forces at Queenston Heights and Frenchman's Creek/Red House in 1812.

2. In 1813 the Americans captured Ft George; but suffered defeat when they tried to advance inland; then were blockaded at Ft George.

3. Late that year the Americans evacuated Ft George and destroyed the civilian towns of Niagara and Queenston; the British captured Ft Niagara and destroyed American property used by the US military.

4. In 1814 the Americans captured Ft Erie, won the battle of Chippawa, but fell back on Ft Erie after the battle of Lundy's Lane to endure a siege before evacuating Canada.

LAKE ONTARIO

NEW YORK

UPPER CANADA

LAKE ERIE

Burlington Beach

Burlington Heights

Stoney Creek

Forty Mile Creek

40 Mile

20 Mile

Grand

Chippawa

Niagara

Ft Niagara

Ft George

Blockade of Ft George

Lewiston

Tuscarora

Queenston

Queenston Heights

Beaver Dams

The Falls

Ft Schlosser

Lundy's Lane

Chippawa

Cook's Mills

Grand Island

Red House

Frenchman's Creek

Siege of Ft Erie

Ft Erie

Caledonia & Detroit

Black Rock

Conjocta Ck

Buffalo

Somers & Ohio

N

0   5 miles

0   10 km

the target. Recognizing the threat, the British deployed men to watch the various routes along which their enemy might advance. As this force continued its march, scouts spotted it and alerted warriors waiting along one of the roads. The tribesmen ambushed the soldiers on 24 June. Despite holding their own for three hours in the fierce battle, the Americans surrendered after concluding that they could not fight their way back to Fort George.

Following this victory, a new British commanding officer in Upper Canada, Major-General Francis de Rottenburg, advanced closer to Fort George to constrict the American foothold in the province further. He did not have enough men to retake the post, so he intended to blockade it until cold weather brought the campaigning season to an end. (The size of the forces fluctuated during the blockade, but generally the British were outnumbered at about 2,000–3,000 against 4,000–5,000 Americans.) De Rottenburg's task was made easier by orders sent from Washington after the recent defeats telling Henry Dearborn to avoid action unless necessary and to concentrate on needed training. Then, in one of his last acts before leaving the Canadian front, Dearborn recruited Haudenosaunee men from reservations in New York who were willing to ally with the US. These men helped to address his light infantry deficiency and counter the warriors opposing his force. Much of the limited amount of success the Americans enjoyed afterwards in pushing back British and Indigenous skirmishers in front of Fort George derived from their efforts. Through the summer that followed, large-scale sorties and raids occurred around the fort on occasion in addition to regular low-level harassment of the American position.

During part of the blockade, the RN squadron cruised the south shore of Lake Ontario to intercept supplies and destroy American depots. Both naval forces on the lake took advantage of such opportunities but evaded a major battle because the consequences of defeat would be devastating for the side that lost control of the strategically important lake. There were some encounters, however.

An important one occurred in August 1813 when each squadron tried to catch its opponent at a disadvantage, but the Americans withdrew from the impending contest after the British captured two schooners and two other US vessels sank during a storm.

As the summer wore on, the British found it increasingly difficult to maintain the blockade at Fort George because of supply problems, widespread sickness, and further losses to their strength as militiamen and warriors drifted away from the front lines. By early October, with General Vincent back in command, they withdrew to comfortable quarters at Burlington Heights, thinking that it was too late in the year for the Americans to pose much of a threat. Yet the invaders unexpectedly made a demonstration towards Burlington but withdrew when they realized how well-entrenched the British were, contenting themselves with burning buildings that their opponents had used closer to Fort George. Soon afterwards, the Americans were no longer in a position to take an aggressive stance on the Niagara Peninsula because they had moved the majority of their troops eastwards to participate in operations against Montreal.

Despite their failures on the Niagara Peninsula, the Americans enjoyed military success in south-western Upper Canada in 1813. After their defeat at Frenchtown, they built Fort Meigs, south of Lake Erie, as a depot and staging point to recapture Michigan and invade Upper Canada. Henry Procter and Tecumseh besieged the fort in late April and early May but could not take it (although losses among US forces were high in comparison to those on the opposing side). A second attempt to capture it in late July also failed. Several days later, another American post in the region, Fort Stephenson, held out against a British attack. Consequently, Procter's men and the warriors who followed Tecumseh retired to the Detroit border region, and the initiative passed to the Americans. On 10 September, the US and British Lake Erie squadrons met for their long-anticipated duel near Put-in-Bay. The British sailed six vessels into battle, while the Americans met them with nine

The 1813 battle of Put-in-Bay, in which the USN had almost twice the firepower of the RN, gave the Americans control of Lake Erie. (Print, c.1816, Yale University Art Gallery, Mabel Brady Garvan Collection)

better-prepared and more heavily armed ships and schooners. Despite the disparities, the battle was close-fought and bloody, but the Americans won, and their commander, Oliver Hazard Perry, could write his famously succinct report: 'We have met the enemy and they are ours: two ships, two brigs, one schooner, and one sloop.'

With this critical loss, and with the Americans still in Fort George at the mouth of the Niagara River, Procter's already tenuous link to the east was cut. Therefore, he destroyed the military works at Detroit and Amherstburg late in September, then retreated eastwards towards

Burlington despite outraged protests from Tecumseh and other Indigenous leaders who wanted to stand and fight. Meanwhile, Perry ferried an American army across the lake. With 3,000 men – including US-allied warriors from the Ohio country – Major-General William Henry Harrison pursued Procter. The invaders caught and defeated 950 soldiers, militiamen, and warriors at Moraviantown on 5 October. Among the slain was Tecumseh. With his death and the recent defeats, Indigenous dreams of achieving an autonomous homeland in the Old Northwest effectively evaporated.

In the weeks that followed, the majority of First Nations survivors from that region went home and made peace with the Americans while others, still willing to fight, sought shelter behind the British lines in the Burlington area.

The western victories formed the only Americans campaign success on the northern front during the conflict and gave them control of part of Upper Canada and most of Lake Erie for the rest of the war. With their triumph at Moraviantown, the road lay open to strike

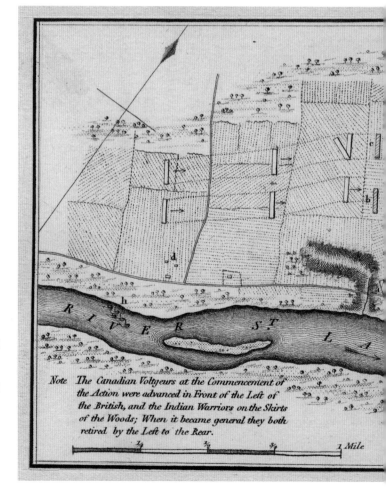

The British defeated the Americans at Crysler's Farm in 1813. The battlefield disappeared when flooded for the St Lawrence Seaway in the 1950s. (Print, 1815, Library and Archives Canada)

Note The Canadian Voltigeurs at the Commencement of the Action were advanced in Front of the Left of the British, and the Indian Warriors on the Skirts of the Woods; When it became general they both retired by the Left to the Rear.

the Haudenosaunee of the Grand River. Its residents, hearing stories of atrocities committed by Americans against Indigenous peoples, fled to join white settlers and Western Tribal refugees in camps behind Burlington Heights. Even there they did not feel safe, thinking that their red-coated allies might retreat to York or Kingston because General Harrison stood poised to use the Grand River to move behind Burlington Heights and attack his enemies. To some extent, the British did not leave because they continued to worry that this might cause a portion

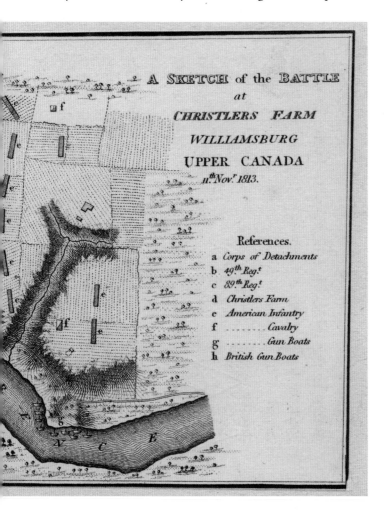

A SKETCH of the BATTLE
at
CHRISTLERS FARM
WILLIAMSBURG
UPPER CANADA
11th Nov.r 1813.

References.

a *Corps of Detachments*
b *49th Reg.t*
c *89th Reg.t*
d *Christlers Farm*
e *American Infantry*
f .... *Cavalry*
g .... *Gun Boats*
h *British Gun Boats*

of their Indigenous allies to join the Americans and turn upon the settlers. Fortunately for them, Harrison was satisfied with his achievements at Moraviantown and chose not to consolidate them with a strike eastwards. Instead, he retired to Amherstburg, dismissed most of his volunteers, and sent the bulk of his regulars to join the army being formed for the Montreal campaign.

Reinforced from Niagara and Detroit, the Americans undertook a two-pronged, 11,000-man offensive against Montreal in their largest operation of the war on the Canadian front. The city was poorly fortified, but the British deployed a sizeable portion of their men to defend its approaches. While one American army marched north from Lake Champlain, another journeyed down the St Lawrence in 325 boats (and made a daring night-time run past the British batteries at Prescott). The first of these forces, commanded by Major-General Wade Hampton, crossed the border south of Montreal, but at Châteauguay on 26 October, 340 well-positioned defenders (consisting mainly of Canadian and First Nations men under Lieutenant-Colonel Charles de Salaberry) repulsed 3,500 of Hampden's soldiers. Then, 11 November, the other thrust, led by Major-General James Wilkinson, ended when 1,200 men under Lieutenant-Colonel Joseph Morrison defeated 3,000 invaders in the open fields of Crysler's Farm beside the St Lawrence River. Hampton and Wilkinson lost their fighting spirit in the aftermath of these disasters and ordered their troops into winter quarters. Thus, ended the most serious threat to the survival of Canada posed by the Americans during the three-year conflict.

There was one more outbreak of fighting along the Canadian border before the close of 1813. With the movement of US troops eastwards to attack Montreal, and with the expiration of many militiamen's terms of service, the American garrison at Fort George dropped to less than 600 soldiers by early December. At that point, and with the passing of Harrison's threat to Burlington, the British wanted to recapture the post. Their opponents, suffering steady harassment, decided to consolidate their forces on the American side of the border. Before withdrawing, their commander, Brigadier-General John McClure, turned the people of the town of Niagara out of their houses in the frigid winter weather and burned down their homes, supposedly to prevent the British from quartering troops there over the winter and to improve Fort Niagara's defensibility across the river from the town. The next day, American artillery at Lewiston fired hot shot at Queenston to set its buildings on fire.

The new British commander in Upper Canada, Lieutenant-General Gordon Drummond, arrived on the peninsula soon afterwards, determined to drive the Americans from the region. His men crossed the Niagara River and made a surprise night assault on the sleeping garrison of Fort Niagara on 19 December. After a short, sharp fight in which the British killed, wounded, or captured all the men of the garrison but lost few of their own, they seized vast quantities of supplies and released prisoners-of-war held at the post. Over the following days, Drummond then cleared his enemies out of the entire New York side of the Niagara area in a series of small victories over the Americans and their Indigenous allies, and in the process set fire to a great many buildings along the river. (Historians usually interpret the devastation as a retaliatory measure for the destruction of Niagara and Queenston, but the residents of the Buffalo area published a little-known but extensive collection of British, Canadian, and American documents in 1817 to prove that the British had burned buildings because they had been used for military purposes, and therefore the settlers thought the government in Washington should compensate them for their losses.) Once Drummond captured Buffalo and destroyed four vessels of the American Lake Erie squadron wintering there, he planned to continue westwards along the south shore of the lake, make a surprise attack on the rest of the squadron anchored at Erie, Pennsylvania, destroy it, and perhaps even retake Detroit. A January thaw, however, rendered the landscape and its rivers impassable, so he abandoned the idea and retired to the Canadian side of

Fort Niagara, captured by the British in December 1813, is one of the war's major Niagara River historic sites today, along with Forts George and Erie. (View Stock / Alamy Stock Photo)

the border, maintaining a garrison on American territory only at Fort Niagara, which the British retained until peace returned in 1815.

The main American objective – the conquest of at least all of Upper Canada – had not been accomplished in 1813, which bought the colony another year's grace. Nevertheless, the Americans emerged from the second year of the war in a better position than they had held in 1812. With a number of victories behind them, they had regained most of their lost territory in the west, occupied a small area of south-western Upper Canada, and seemed to have removed the possibility of an Indigenous homeland being created at their expense in part of the Old Northwest.

1814

Great Britain's inability to send significant numbers of soldiers and sailors to fight the Americans changed with the defeat of France in the spring of 1814. In March, British and allied forces marched into Paris, followed by Napoleon's abdication in April, whereupon the government in London began sending far more men west across the Atlantic than it had before. As the new campaigning season approached with the end of the cold weather, the Americans needed to take advantage of the following few months before most of these reinforcements reached Canada. They recognized that the conquest of all of the colonies on their northern border was no longer possible, but they hoped to secure an advantageous position for peace negotiations in hopes of annexing Upper Canada and mitigating any threats to their own territory that might occur elsewhere, such as could happen if the British were to occupy part of New England.

Logically, their 1814 strategy should have concentrated on the early capture of Kingston or Montreal with the aim of cutting off the upper province. Instead, they chose to direct their efforts in the west, partly because the battles of Lake Erie and Moraviantown gave them dominance there, which they strengthened further by reoccupying Buffalo after Gordon Drummond abandoned it during the winter. The Madison administration also decided to target two distinct regions on the northern border rather than one. The government directed one army to cross the Niagara River from Buffalo, march up the Niagara Peninsula, drive out the British, and then continue as far east as possible, ideally seizing all of Upper Canada. It ordered a second force to sail north from Detroit to retake Mackinac at the head of Lake Michigan. This decision was a mistake because it diverted resources away from the Niagara front that could have given the Americans a decisive numerical advantage over their opponents in a closely fought campaign.

Before these plans could be put into effect, there were several notable confrontations along the Great Lakes border as the two sides tried to achieve advantages before the upcoming campaigns began. In February, the British raided American communities along the St Lawrence River to take supplies. In March, an American army marched against Montreal, but withdrew when it could not dislodge a small force at Lacolle. In May,

A British officer recorded the 1814 attack on Oswego first-hand, depicting troops transferring to boats from the Lake Ontario squadron to capture the American post. (Watercolour, 1814, Library of Congress)

the British captured Oswego, but an attempt later that month to seize naval supplies at Sandy Creek resulted in defeat, and then they cancelled a planned attack on the US Navy's base at Sackett's Harbour because they did not have enough men for the assault.

The American expedition against Mackinac called for the recapture of the post and the destruction of British military and fur trade facilities in the north. The objectives were to regain the lost fort, force the northern First Nations out of the war, and halt the flow of supplies to the tribes along the upper Mississippi, who continued fighting despite the withdrawal of many of their compatriots farther east who had participated in Tecumseh's alliance. The Americans had expected that their successes in south-western Upper Canada would have cut the supply line to these areas. The British, however, overcame the loss of Lake Erie to some extent by sending supplies to Mackinac from Montreal via the traditional fur trade route that extended up the Ottawa River and along other waterways to Lake Huron, and by moving materiel west through Kingston to York, then north by road, water, and portage to Georgian Bay and points in the west. Neither route allowed them to send as much as they could have done via Lake Erie if it had remained open to them, so shortages in the north were severe, but enough got through to maintain their presences in this isolated theatre and supply Indigenous allies across the upper lakes and along the Mississippi.

About 1,000 regulars, militia, and sailors on five vessels of the US Lake Erie squadron travelled into Lake Huron in July 1814 under the command of Lieutenant-Colonel George Croghan of the army and Captain Arthur Sinclair of the navy. On their way to Mackinac, they captured two commercial vessels as well as a number of bateaux, and burned the abandoned British post on St Joseph's Island and fur-trade buildings on the St Mary's River. They landed on Mackinac Island on 4 August, planning to advance against the fort. Its commandant, Lieutenant-Colonel Robert McDouall, marched out from his defences with 550 soldiers, militia, and warriors to defeat the invaders. With this loss, the American commanders sent two vessels south with their sick and wounded, and then sailed the others to Georgian Bay, where the Americans destroyed a blockhouse and the schooner *Nancy*, although its 17-man Royal Navy crew escaped. Then, one of the three remaining American vessels returned to Lake Erie, while the schooners *Tigress* and *Scorpion* headed west to blockade Mackinac. The men from the *Nancy* set out for Mackinac in two bateaux and a canoe, accompanied by warriors and fur traders. They slipped past the blockade and obtained permission to try to seize the American vessels. Reinforced with four boats and 50 soldiers, they surprised and captured the *Tigress* in hand-to-hand fighting on 3 September. Three days later, they sailed their prize up to the unsuspecting *Scorpion*, opened fire, boarded, and captured the vessel. Thus, in small-scale fighting, the British kept control over the vast northern regions before the first snows of the winter of 1814–15 began to fall, thereby also retaining the ability to supply their allies in the Mississippi country. Nevertheless, the damage to the fur trade infrastructure exacerbated the already grim supply problems faced by the people in these regions.

The British captured Fort Mackinac in 1812, then defended it in 1814. Today it is a heritage site interpreting military history from the 1780s to the 1890s. (Layne Kennedy/ Getty Images)

The main American offensive came from Buffalo with a better-trained and -officered force than any the United States had deployed so far in the war. Two years of frustration had led to the replacement of many of their poor-quality senior leaders, and the army had benefited from rigorous training designed to overcome its earlier deficiencies. On 3 July 1814, Major-General Jacob Brown brought 5,000 soldiers and 600 warriors across the south end of the Niagara River against Fort Erie. The 150-man garrison resisted for 14 hours before surrendering. When the British commander on the Niagara front, Major-General Phineas Riall (headquartered towards the north end of the river), heard about the invasion – but not about the fall of the fort – he rushed south towards Chippawa where he expected to repel Brown. He also sent some of his Indigenous allies and light troops further south to watch American movements and delay any attempt to move north.

On 4 July, one of Brown's brigades, commanded by Brigadier-General Winfield Scott, advanced north with the objective of seizing the bridge across the Chippawa (now Welland) River; Riall's skirmishers harassed their enemy as they withdrew and destroyed the bridge and nearby buildings that might provide cover for the Americans. They then retired to the north bank of the Chippawa. Faced with the loss of the bridge and opposed by a British battery on the far shore, Scott withdrew and camped along the south bank of Street's (now Usher's) Creek. There, the American right flank anchored on the Niagara River, while their left rested 1,200 yards (1,100m) across fields at the edge of a forest. During the night and the next day, the other two brigades in Brown's army arrived in the camp.

Riall underestimated the size of the force opposing him because part of the American army arrived in their camp after his patrols had performed a reconnaissance of his enemy's lines and because he did not realize that Fort Erie had capitulated, so he assumed that some of Brown's troops were investing the place. On 5 July, with 1,800 men, he decided to attack Brown, who deployed 2,100 soldiers and warriors against him. Riall sent his light infantry, Canadian militia, and Indigenous allies through the woods to attack the American left. Meanwhile, he organized the rest of his regulars to advance across the plain beside the Niagara River, but without the Americans realizing what he planned to do because the topography hid his crossing of the Chippawa River. General Brown, unaware of Riall's movements to his front, already had decided to put an end to the minor harassment he had been enduring from small groups of warriors in the forest on his left, and so he sent one of his brigades, consisting of regulars, volunteers, and First Nations allies, into the bush to clear out the skirmishers. In the ensuing encounter, the brigade inflicted heavy casualties upon the British-allied warriors but was repelled when it came up against the light force that Riall had deployed as part of the main attack. From the sound of the firing in the forest, Brown assumed that he was about to be attacked in front, so he deployed his men to meet the soon-to-become-visible British troops advancing across the plain. Jacob Brown and Phineas Riall clashed in a classic linear battle. The combined fire of the American artillery and musketry halted the British advance. A stationary, close-range struggle ensued for the next 20 minutes, with the Americans holding up better than they had in comparable battles earlier in the war. Then, Riall, realizing he had been defeated, ordered a retreat.

Afterwards, both armies returned to their former positions: the British on the north side of the Chippawa River, the Americans on the south side of Street's Creek. Riall then fell back to the mouth of the Niagara River on 8 July, where the British were well entrenched, occupying Forts George and Niagara, as well as a new work, Fort Mississauga, then under construction. Brown marched to Queenston Heights, established a camp, probed the British works to the north, and awaited the arrival of the USN's Lake Ontario squadron to push his adversaries out of the peninsula. Afterwards, he expected the navy to transport his men against York and Kingston. He needed to be cautious until the navy appeared, however, because the British not only garrisoned troops in the three forts but stationed men at Burlington Heights and the mouth of Forty Mile Creek on Lake Ontario who might attempt to swing behind his rear.

Despite pre-arranged plans, Commodore Chauncey did not sail his squadron to Brown's assistance. Instead, he sent a variety of excuses to account for his inaction, even declaring that the navy had a higher calling than that of merely supporting the army. Without Chauncey, and facing losses in his ranks because of sickness, while the British began to receive reinforcements from Europe, Brown decided to retire southwards. The British marched against the Americans, and the two armies met at dusk on 25 July at Lundy's Lane, close to Niagara Falls. There, 2,800 Americans fought 3,500 men opposite them to a bloody standstill in the confusion of the dark, with

The 1814 battle of Lundy's Lane largely occurred in the dark, which, combined with thick gun smoke, made it difficult to identify friends from enemies. (Print, 1815, Library of Congress)

the opposing lines pouring devastating volleys into each other from distances as short as 15 paces. At the end, the Americans briefly held the field, but then withdrew back to Fort Erie. The British, badly bloodied, could not pursue them right away, which gave Brown time to improve the defences of a camp attached to the fort to house his forces. At the same time, the US Lake Ontario squadron finally arrived, which restricted the British from advancing south for a time because of the threat it posed to their rear and because it stopped supplies being sent from Kingston. Nevertheless, from a strategic perspective, Lundy's Lane was a British victory because they halted the invasion and because the initiative on the Niagara Peninsula shifted from the invaders to the defenders.

This plan shows Fort Erie in 1814, its additional fortified American camp (left), and the British siege lines in the forest (far right). (Print, 1816, Courtesy of the John Carter Brown Library, CC BY-SA 4.0)

Gordon Drummond, who had resumed command on the Niagara Peninsula just before the battle of Lundy's Lane, moved against Fort Erie early in August and put it under blockade. Unlike Francis de Rottenburg outside Fort George in 1813, he intended to retake the post rather than just keep the Americans inside until the coming of cold weather. This was a poor decision because Brown's force was still strong and because the Americans could ferry supplies and reinforcements to the fort from Buffalo because a British attempt against the town, initiated from Fort Niagara, had been repulsed at Conjocta Creek to the north of the settlement. During the blockade, Drummond launched an assault against Fort Erie during the darkness of the early hours of 15 August.

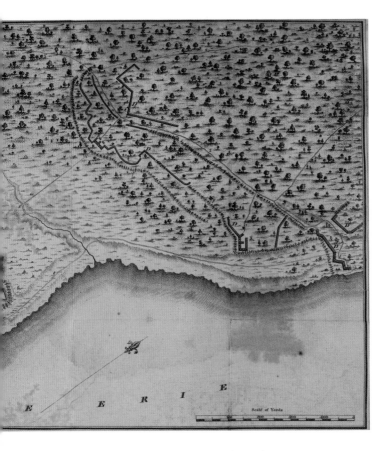

It was meant to be a surprise, but the Americans were waiting. Consequently, the attack cost the British heavily in killed, wounded, and prisoners taken. After more fighting, the British, frustrated and facing supply problems, sickness, and bad weather, decided to abandon the blockade. While they prepared to leave, the Americans sortied from the fort on 17 September, spiked three of Drummond's six siege guns, and destroyed ammunition. Each side lost over 500 men killed, wounded and missing in that encounter, exceeding the casualties endured at the famous battle of Chippewa, in part because the opposing armies were receiving substantial numbers of reinforcements as the summer came to an end. In the aftermath of the clash, Drummond retired northwards.

In October, the Americans marched north from Fort Erie in a final attempt to gain territory beyond the south-western corner of Upper Canada and the grounds immediately around the fort that they then occupied. At Cook's Mills, British troops bloodied, but did not defeat their advanced detachments; however, the Americans withdrew back to the fort. Meanwhile, in an initiative to deprive the British of foodstuffs and subdue the population of south-western Upper Canada, the Americans raided along the Lake Erie shoreline with 720 men under Brigadier-General Duncan McArthur late in the year and hoped to come to Brown's aid at Fort Erie. The expedition faltered when it came up against Haudenosaunee resistance at the Grand River, and so turned back towards Detroit. Nevertheless, the Americans won a small victory at Malcolm's Mills and destroyed mills, farms, and supplies that Drummond had hoped would meet some of his army's needs over the coming winter.

By this time, it was not possible to think of seizing any more of Upper Canada because the British now controlled Lake Ontario. Their success did not occur in a dramatic naval confrontation, but through the labours of shipbuilders who, in September, launched the 104-gun ship-of-the-line, HMS *St Lawrence*. The now powerful RN squadron put the USN under blockade at Sackett's Harbour. With little prospect of expelling the British from the Niagara Peninsula, and none of advancing farther east, the Americans blew up Fort Erie on 5 November and retired to Buffalo. Thus, the 1814 American Niagara and Mackinac campaigns came to a failed end, despite impressive tactical successes on the Niagara Peninsula. With the exception of a small area in south-western Upper Canada lost in 1813, the British North American colonies survived the third year of the war.

The war on the upper Mississippi

In a vast area that historians often overlook in relation to the War of 1812, fighting on the upper Mississippi

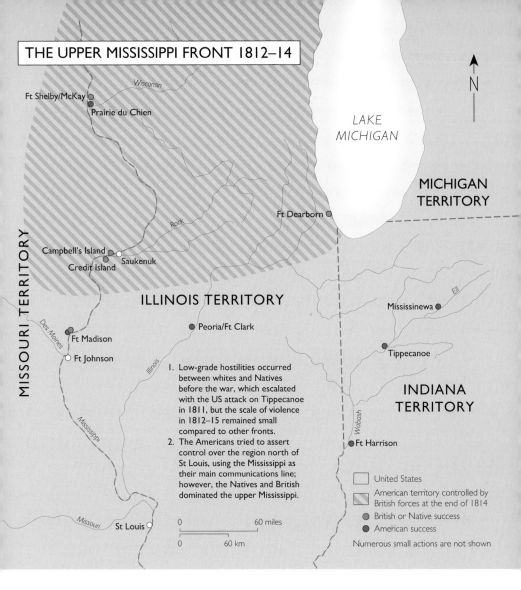

THE UPPER MISSISSIPPI FRONT 1812–14

Wisconsin

Ft Shelby/McKay
Prairie du Chien

LAKE
MICHIGAN

N

MICHIGAN
TERRITORY

Rock

Ft Dearborn

MISSOURI TERRITORY

Campbell's Island
Credit Island
Saukenuk

ILLINOIS TERRITORY

Mississinewa

Eel

Des Moines

Ft Madison
Ft Johnson

Peoria/Ft Clark

Tippecanoe

Illinois

INDIANA
TERRITORY

Wabash

1. Low-grade hostilities occurred
between whites and Natives
before the war, which escalated
with the US attack on Tippecanoe
in 1811, but the scale of violence
in 1812–15 remained small
compared to other fronts.

2. The Americans tried to assert
control over the region north of
St Louis, using the Mississippi as
their main communications line;
however, the Natives and British
dominated the upper Mississippi.

Ft Harrison

Mississippi

☐ United States
▨ American territory controlled by
British forces at the end of 1814
● British or Native success
● American success

Numerous small actions are not shown

Missouri   St Louis

0   60 miles

0   60 km

River saw Indigenous and American forces clash over the
future of the region. The First Nations there, like others
on the frontiers of the United States, wanted to preserve
their territories and independence, whereas Americans
sought to acquire their lands for the benefit of settler
society. Unlike the situation farther east where warriors
had gathered around Tecumseh, the main threat to the
tribes of the upper Mississippi came north from St Louis,
as exemplified by a fraudulent treaty imposed on them

there in 1804 by William Henry Harrison that alienated massive tracts of Sauk, Mesquakie (or Fox), and other territories in today's Missouri, Illinois, and Wisconsin. While hundreds of Mississippi warriors fought elsewhere during the conflict, including alongside Tecumseh, the war in their homelands essentially was a separate struggle, despite similar concerns and behaviours. As occurred elsewhere, many Indigenous people went to war with the United States, some chose neutrality, and a small number aligned with the Americans. The British contributed to this struggle by sending modest quantities of men and supplies to aid their allies.

As early as 1809, tensions became obvious when the Americans built Fort Bellevue (later Madison) on the Mississippi River. Indigenous people threatened to destroy it because they resented this attempt by the United States to extend its authority onto their lands. As it was, the surrounding territory suffered from low-grade violence between the First Nations and settler populations, marked by robberies, assaults, and murders committed by both sides. With the coming of war, settlers and Indigenous people moved away from each other for their safety while violence began to escalate as groups of individuals, militiamen, and war parties raided and burned their adversaries' villages, and as both sides committed atrocities against non-combatants. American settlers and soldiers also responded by building fortifications, either to protect themselves or to project power into the contested territory.

The first notable confrontation in the region occurred between 5 and 8 September 1812 when Indigenous warriors besieged Fort Madison but failed to take it. The second year of the war, however, did not see another major clash, but a continuation of raids and skirmishes similar to those of 1811 and 1812, although a significant number of Sauks and Mesquakies who preferred neutrality left their lands around modern Davenport, Iowa to move south to the Missouri River where they thought they would be safer. There was a long-standing French-Canadian fur trade presence in the region with close connections to the Indigenous population, which generated considerable distrust among anglophone Americans. Therefore, as US forces destroyed neighbouring First Nations communities in November 1813, they also burned the francophone settlement of Peoria because they thought its residents had aided the Kickapoos, Potawatomis, and Piankashaws against them. One of the more meaningful events of 1813 on the upper Mississippi occurred during the same month when the Americans burned and abandoned Fort Madison after enduring months of harassment that led them to believe that holding the post through the winter would be impossible.

In 1814, the Americans escalated the scale of hostilities by making concerted efforts to win control of the upper Mississippi by sending troops upriver from St Louis in fortified gunboats and other watercraft. In the spring, they intimidated the Indigenous people along the way into a temporary peace, seized the fur trade village Prairie du Chien in early June and built Fort Shelby beside it. Their adversaries, however, rose against the invaders, and, supported by reinforcements from Mackinac, retook the village and forced the surrender of the fort in a siege between 17 and 20 July, after which the post was renamed Fort McKay. On 21 July, war parties to the south, some led by the famous Sauk chief Black Hawk, attacked the gunboat flotilla at Campbell's Island and drove it downriver. The flotilla, with 430 men, returned in September to destroy Indigenous villages and contest control over the region. However, 1,000 Sauk, Mesquakie, Winnebago, Sioux, and other warriors, with a small contingent of Euro-Americans, defeated it at Credit Island on 5 September, again forcing it to withdraw southwards after artillery shot from a British 3-pounder kept penetrating the boats and inflicting casualties while the large numbers of warriors on shore prevented the Americans from landing soldiers to attack the gun. As a result, the tribespeople and their British allies exercised control over much of the upper Mississippi in the final months of the war, with advanced

This naïve image of upper Mississippi people includes a Black man, whose presence documents some of the diversity existing within the period's Indigenous populations. (Watercolour, 1814, Library and Archives Canada)

American positions being limited to Fort Clark at Peoria and Fort Johnson near the junction of the Mississippi and Des Moines rivers. Small-scale violence continued into 1815, and the final peace negotiations between the region's First Nations and the United States did not

conclude until 1817. Afterwards, continuing pressures by land-hungry settlers led to another outburst of violence in 1832, in a series of grim confrontations known as the Black Hawk War that confirmed post-war American dominance over the area.

The saltwater war

With the approach of war, the American government deployed the US Navy on the Atlantic Ocean to guard merchantmen on their return home, seize British commercial vessels, and hunt for Royal Navy ships. It was at that early point that the Americans chased HMS *Belvidera* to Halifax, mentioned above, which led the British squadron there to sail forth in response. In mid-July 1812, the British sighted and captured the American brig USS *Nautilus* without a fight. Soon afterwards, they came into contact with the USS *Constitution,* but the frigate escaped after a tension-filled multi-day chase. A few weeks later, the American frigate *Essex* overwhelmed the smaller Royal Navy sloop *Alert* in a short engagement near the Grand Banks of Newfoundland. These first encounters defined the fundamental characteristics of high seas confrontations between the two navies for the rest of the conflict: in most situations, bigger and better-armed ships captured their opponents without a fight, lost them in a chase, or defeated them in combat. Occasionally, however, the two navies met on near-equal terms. The best-known of these incidents occurred in June 1813, when the USS *Chesapeake* ventured out from Boston to meet HMS *Shannon*. Of these two frigates, the *Shannon* had a smaller crew, but its captain had devoted years to developing his men's gunnery skills. The *Chesapeake* was a better-built vessel, but the crew included a large number of newcomers, some experienced, others not. After 15 minutes of horror, including hand-to-hand fighting and heavy casualties as a boarding party descended on the *Chesapeake*, the Americans surrendered.

The most famous warship of the conflict was the USS *Constitution*, one of the American heavy frigates. After escaping from the British squadron, its crew defeated the frigates *Guerrière* and *Java* respectively in August and December 1812 and inflicted so much damage that the American commander decided to sink both RN ships rather than try to salvage them for use by the USN. Although blockaded in port for much of 1813

THE OCEAN WAR BETWEEN THE USN AND THE RN 1812–15

GREAT BRITAIN

NORTH AMERICA

AFRICA

CARIBBEAN SEA

SOUTH AMERICA

ATLANTIC OCEAN

PACIFIC OCEAN

● British success
● American success

Note: US ships are named first

1812
1. *Nautilus* captured by a RN squadron
2. *Essex* vs *Alert*
3. *Constitution* vs *Guerrière*
4. *Wasp* vs *Frolic*
5. *Wasp* and *Frolic* captured by *Poictiers*
6. *United States* vs *Macedonian*
7. *Vixen* captured by *Southampton*
8. *Constitution* vs *Java*

1813
9. *Viper* captured by *Narcissus*
10. *Hornet* vs *Peacock*
11. *Chesapeake* vs *Shannon*
12. *Argus* vs *Pelican*
13. *Enterprise* vs *Boxer*
14. *Vixen II* captured by *Belvidera*

1814
15. *Constitution* captured *Pictou*
16. *Essex* and *Essex Junior* vs *Phoebe* and *Cherub*
17. *Frolic* captured by *Orpheus* and *Shelburne*
18. *Peacock* vs *Epervier*
19. *Rattlesnake* captured by *Leander*
20. *Wasp II* vs *Reindeer*
21. *Syren* captured by *Medway*
22. *Wasp II* vs *Avon*

1815
23. *President* vs RN squadron
24. *Constitution* vs *Levant* and *Cyane*
25. *Levant* recaptured by RN squadron
26. *Hornet* vs *Penguin*

Map does not include warships that escaped from larger forces, coastal and freshwater operations, actions involving privateers, or the seizure of merchantmen.

and 1814, the *Constitution* escaped for a cruise in early 1814 and captured and destroyed a schooner, HMS *Pictou*. Then, in February 1815, it met two smaller British warships, the corvette *Cyane* and the sloop *Levant*, defeated both in a single action, and managed to get the *Cyane* back to the United States after being chased by a squadron of Royal Navy warships, which recaptured the other vessel.

An important aspect of the naval conflict was the effort made by the British and American governments to use their warships against merchantmen. The British, in particular, also organized convoys to diminish threats to their commercial vessels. One well-known instance of commerce raiding occurred in the summer of 1813, when the USN brig *Argus* ventured into the home waters of the United Kingdom. Merchant ships were vulnerable there because convoys typically broke up near the end of their journeys as individual vessels sailed to different ports, and because the RN deployed much of its strength to blockade enemies rather than guard the British Isles. The *Argus* took 19 merchantmen over three weeks, burning most of them, until HMS *Pelican* captured it in mid-August. In another cruise, the USS *Essex* severely weakened the British South Pacific whaling industry when the frigate captured many of the vessels engaged in the business. In this war against commercial shipping, the USN seized 172 British commercial ships (and a few troop transports), while the Royal Navy captured 1,407 American merchant vessels.

In addition to the commerce raiding of their navies, both Great Britain and the United States licensed privateers to seize enemy ships for profit in a kind of legalized piracy. Some of these privately owned vessels were fast-sailing and heavily crewed, being designed to prey upon slower, lightly manned merchantmen. Others were regular ships that attempted to seize vessels when opportunities arose during their normal round of business. Privateering was a perilous business: of 526 known American vessels that engaged in this form of commercial warfare, 278 were captured and many were lost to British action, but only 207 took a prize. Some of the privateers seized by the British entered Royal Navy service, although the RN lost a handful of small vessels to larger privateers. British privateers, largely from the North American maritime colonies, seized several hundred prizes, especially among coastal trading craft. American privately owned ships captured 1,600 merchantmen from the richer pickings of the British Empire. However, of the vessels taken by American privateers and warships, at least 750 either were recaptured by the British, handed back by neutral powers, or lost at sea, often being burned by their captors after they removed valuable cargoes because there was little chance of getting them home in the face of RN patrols. Other captured ships were used to return prisoners, and the owners of American privateers ransomed a significant number of their prizes back to their owners.

The USS *United States* captured HMS *Macedonian* in 1812. Launched in 1797, it was one of America's heavy frigates that usually outclassed opposing frigates. (Print, 1813, National Portrait Gallery, Smithsonian Institution; gift of the McNeil Americana Collection, CC0)

In 1813, HMS *Shannon* captured the USS *Chesapeake*. As was common on both sides, the victors added their prize to their own navy. (Oil, c.1813, © Chicago History Museum / Bridgeman Images)

The event that had the greatest impact on the ocean war was the Royal Navy's blockade of the American coast. It began informally in 1812 with the modest resources available in the western Atlantic at that time. Then, as more warships could be deployed against the United States, the RN cut off a larger number of ports from the outside world. In February 1813, the blockade covered the region between Delaware and Chesapeake bays, where public enthusiasm for the war was greater than in other seafaring communities. In March 1813, the navy expanded the blockade to include Savannah, Port Royal, Charleston, and New York, then extended it again by mid-November to the entire coast south of Narragansett Bay. Yet, the British exempted most of New England until late in the conflict because they hoped to increase dissension between its states, which opposed hostilities, and the rest of the country, and because their army fighting the French in Spain and Portugal needed American grain to survive, which New England merchants and others supplied in ships licensed and protected by the British. In May 1814, with Napoleon defeated in Europe and the end of the army's Iberian supply problems, the RN then blockaded New England with warships provisioned and maintained from bases in Newfoundland, Nova Scotia, Bermuda, and the West Indies (and these vessels purchased additional supplies from profit-seeking Americans in US coastal waters).

One consequence of the expanding blockade was that the USN could not get its vessels out to sea with ease. For example, the heavy frigate *United States* and two smaller warships set sail to seize British West Indian shipping in 1813 but fled back to port when a Royal Navy squadron intercepted them. They then remained immobile for the rest of the conflict, as did six new heavy frigates and four larger ships-of-the-line that the Americans built during the war. The British not only prevented much of the USN's saltwater fleet from leaving port but dissuaded many privateers as well. Despite the tightening noose, some vessels managed to evade the blockade to fight the RN or raid British commerce.

Most importantly, the blockade devastated America's international trade. Between 1811, the last full year of peace, and 1814, the value of American exports and imports fell from $114 million to $20 million, and customs revenues, used to finance the war, fell from $13 million to $6 million (despite a doubling of the rates). At the same time, the cost of trade within the country's borders increased markedly because people abandoned the efficient but now-dangerous coastal lanes for slow overland routes. By 1814, only one out of every 12 merchant ships in the United States dared leave port, plainly exemplifying the economic impact of the war on the republic's economy. For the British, in contrast, international trade grew in the same period, from £91 million in 1811 to £152 million in 1814, despite American actions that brought death, destruction, and heartache to the people of the British maritime world.

The United States under attack

Beginning in February 1813, British army and naval commanders used modest reinforcements from Europe to launch destructive raids against the Chesapeake region close to Washington. They usually met ineffectual resistance as they attacked military, naval, maritime, and industrial targets, and captured large numbers of private and government vessels. They also burned or took property when civilians offered resistance or did not offer ransoms against the seizure or destruction of strategically valuable possessions (although those who remained quietly at home normally were left alone and were paid for supplies requisitioned to support British operations). Raids took place elsewhere along the Atlantic coast, notably in areas where the population undertook hostile acts against the blockades. Among the several dozen operations, most of which were successful, six boats from a blockading naval force rowed up the Connecticut River in April 1814 to torch seven privateers, 12 ocean-going merchantmen, and ten coastal vessels at Pettipaug (now Essex).

With troops freed from the late European war, the British expanded their operations against the American Atlantic coast. In addition to the small raids of earlier months, they undertook raids in strength (which often have been misinterpreted as invasions). In August, they landed several thousand men near Washington, and on the 22nd, Royal Marines and sailors struck at the American gunboat flotilla on the Patuxent River. The Americans lost a privateer, 17 gunboats, and 13 merchant schooners, either destroyed by retreating US forces or seized by their opponents. On 24 August, 4,000 men from the overall British contingent marched on Washington, defeating 6,000 militia, seamen, and regulars at Bladensburg on their way to the capital. Among those who retreated from the battlefield as quickly as he could was James Madison.

BRITISH ATLANTIC COUNTER-ATTACK 1812–14

Quebec

LOWER CANADA

NEW BRUNSWICK

MASS (Maine)

Halifax

NOVA SCOTIA

Eastport
Bangor
Machias
Montreal
Belfast
Castine
Hampden
Ottawa

UPPER CANADA

VT

NH

Boston

MASSACHUSETTS

NEW YORK

RI

Hartford
CT
Pettipaug

New York

ATLANTIC OCEAN

PENNSYLVANIA

NEW JERSEY

Philadelphia

Havre de Grace
North Point
Baltimore
Bladensburg
DEL
Washington
Kent Is
Alexandria
Pig Point
Ft Washington
MD

Royal Navy Blockade

VIRGINIA

Hampton
Craney Is

NORTH CAROLINA

SOUTH CAROLINA

Charleston

Savannah

GEORGIA

EAST FLORIDA

E

D

C

A

B

A

C

D

British territory
United States
American territory controlled by British forces at the end of 1814
British success
American success
Areas of concentrated British raids
Numerous small actions are not shown

RN BLOCKADE
A. Jan 1813: Delaware and Chesapeake bays
B. Feb 1813: extended between Delaware and Chesapeake
C. Mar 1813: extended to New York and points south of the Chesapeake
D. Nov 1813: extended to entire coast south of Narragansett Bay
E. May 1814: extended to entire Atlantic coast

Note: before 1813, blockading occurred, but was limited, based on available ships.

1. As ships became available, the RN extended its blockade to cripple US international trade and reduce the capability of the USN and privateers to get their ships out of port.

2. In 1813–14, the British made dozens of largely successful raids to help draw the war away from the Great Lakes, retaliate for US actions in Canada, and speed the peace process.

3. The end of the war in Europe in 1814 allowed the British to undertake more ambitious operations against modern Maine and the Chesapeake region.

N

0   100 miles
0   200 km

Meanwhile the president's wife, Dolley (or Dolly), saved what she could from the presidential mansion, including a famous portrait of George Washington attributed to Gilbert Stuart. As the British advanced on the capital, the commandant of the Washington navy yard burned its extensive facilities as well as a frigate and a sloop, while other people blew up a fort at nearby Greenleaf's Point. The victorious redcoats entered the capital unopposed and set fire to government buildings and military facilities. They also seized remarkable quantities of munitions and weapons before starting back to their ships the next day. Reflecting on the American occupation in York a year earlier, the governor-in-chief of British North America, Sir George Prevost, wrote that 'as a just retribution, the proud capital at Washington has experienced a similar fate to that inflicted by an American force on the seat of government in Upper Canada.' Meanwhile, other British soldiers and sailors moved upriver against Fort Washington. Expecting a fight, they were surprised when the Americans blew

In 1814, the British burned the White House, Congress, some of Washington's other public buildings, and military targets, but left most private property alone. (Print, 1815, Everett Collection Inc / Alamy Stock Photo)

up their defences and retreated. The British then took Alexandria on 27–29 August and seized goods and prize vessels. As the squadron withdrew, the Americans prepared shore batteries to destroy the British ships, but the raiders had little trouble opposing them on their way back to sea by early September.

The British then moved against Baltimore, home of much of the privateering fleet. The navy moved to the mouth of the Patapsco River on 11 September and landed troops the next day. The soldiers marched against the city in a demonstration that might be turned into a real assault if resistance proved to be inadequate. Meanwhile, the men on the naval vessels began preparations to attack the harbour defences. On the way, the soldiers on land came under fire at North Point but drove their enemy away. However, their commanding officer, Major-General Robert Ross, the victor of Bladensburg, fell mortally wounded in the battle. On 13 September, they marched closer to Baltimore, but were unable to progress into the city when they encountered an overwhelmingly large force of well-entrenched Americans. Nevertheless, pessimists in the city burned the ropewalks that supplied the city's ships and schooners along with a new USN frigate. Meanwhile, the Royal Navy engaged Forts Covington and McHenry for 25 hours over 13–14 September with bombs and rockets from such evocatively named ships as *Volcano*, *Aetna*, and *Meteor*. The fleet, however, could not get close enough to its targets to do much damage, partly because Baltimoreans had sunk 24 merchant vessels to block the way as part of their heroic efforts to prepare the community's defences. Meanwhile, American gunboats threatened the squadron's rear. Despite some continued fighting, the British commander, Vice-Admiral Sir Alexander Cochrane, decided to withdraw, and the officers on land called off an assault because the odds against them were far too steep to expect to succeed. Although defeated at North Point, the Americans were jubilant. Their forts had held out and Baltimore had been saved.

With reinforcement from Europe, the British sent troops from Nova Scotia to occupy the Maine district of Massachusetts. They first took Moose Island and its fort on 11–12 July 1814, then Castine and Belfast on 1 September. Two days later, they attacked Hampden and dispersed its defenders. During that action, the Americans burned a corvette to prevent its capture. On 5 September, the British marched into Bangor and took a large number of merchant vessels, and then seized Machias soon afterwards.

With reinforcements sent to Lower Canada, the governor-in-chief of British North America, Sir George Prevost, invaded northern New York. He marched south late in the summer of 1814 with 10,000 men, intending to capture the border community of Plattsburgh on Lake Champlain to help secure Lower Canada's vulnerable frontier. However, the United States Navy had built a formidable squadron on the lake. He believed it would need to be destroyed before he could move against the town because he did not think it would be safe to operate with such a force on his flank and rear. He ordered the British squadron on the lake into action on 11 September, although its commanding officer did not think it ready to do so, but hoped that support from the general directed against American land-based batteries would give him victory. The British naval force carrying 100 guns met the US squadron, armed with 86, supported by additional artillery from the shore batteries. About an hour after the lake battle began, Prevost ordered his army to advance on Plattsburgh itself, but he left the batteries alone. Half an hour later, the British squadron was defeated, and its commander, George Downie, lay dead under an overturned 24-pounder. Prevost, unwilling to continue with the American squadron threatening his back, or suffer heavy casualties out of proportion to the strategic value of Plattsburgh, cancelled the attack and withdrew to Canada. His officers were outraged but the Americans were delighted, rewarding their naval commander, Thomas Macdonough, with praise and a promotion as one of their country's greatest heroes.

The British occupied Castine in New England in 1814–15. Note the fort on high ground, circular batteries elsewhere, and the civilian town. (Manuscript detail, 1815, Library and Archives Canada)

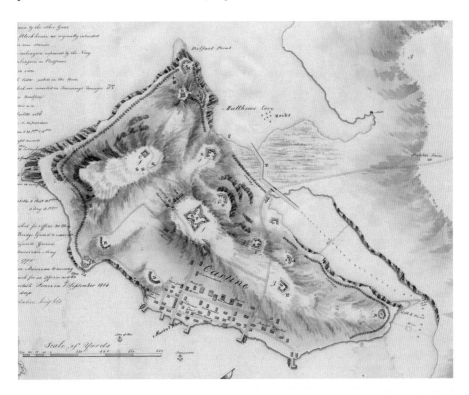

Towards the end of the conflict, far to the south of the Great Lakes, the British attacked the American Gulf coast. Until that time, the region had played few roles in the Anglo-American crisis, but the United States engaged in two parallel conflicts in the area. Spain ruled East and West Florida but could not devote much attention to these colonies because of the war to expel the French army from its own homeland. In 1810 and 1812, the United States annexed parts of West Florida and sent troops to occupy part of the colony. (In 1819, Spain ceded East Florida and renounced its claims to West Florida in a treaty outside of the context of the War of 1812.) To the north, the people of the Muscogee confederacy fought a terrible civil war among themselves in 1813–14, mainly in today's Alabama, over whether they should sell land and adapt to Euro-American ways. The violence brought American intervention when traditionalists attacked white settlers, and the subsequent

In 1814, the USN's Lake Champlain squadron of four sailing vessels and ten gunboats and galleys defeated the Royal Navy's four vessels and 15 gunboats. (Print, 1816, Library of Congress)

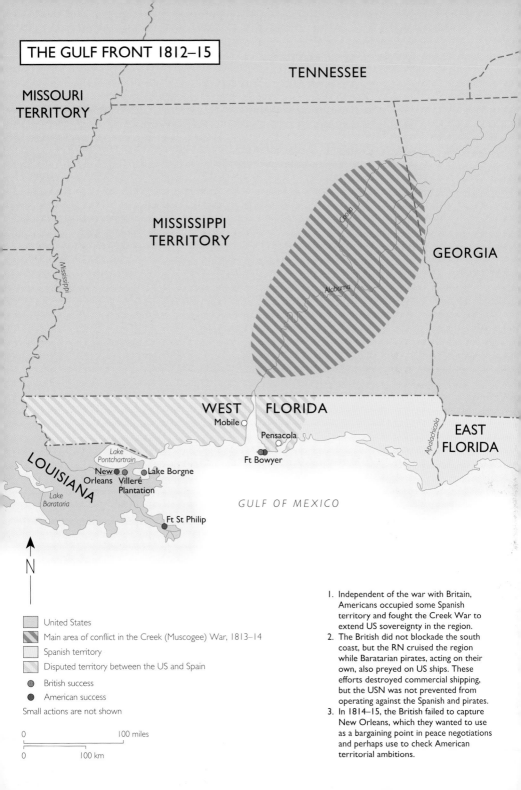

THE GULF FRONT 1812–15

MISSOURI
TERRITORY

TENNESSEE

MISSISSIPPI
TERRITORY

GEORGIA

Mississippi

Coosa

Alabama

WEST   FLORIDA

Mobile ○

Pensacola ●

Ft Bowyer ●●

EAST
FLORIDA

Apalachicola

Lake Pontchartrain

LOUISIANA

New ●● ○ Lake Borgne
Orleans Villeré
          Plantation

Lake Baratarai

Ft St Philip ●

GULF OF MEXICO

N

0 _____ 100 miles

0 _____ 100 km

☐ United States
▨ Main area of conflict in the Creek (Muscogee) War, 1813–14
☐ Spanish territory
▨ Disputed territory between the US and Spain
● British success
● American success
Small actions are not shown

1. Independent of the war with Britain,
   Americans occupied some Spanish
   territory and fought the Creek War to
   extend US sovereignty in the region.
2. The British did not blockade the south
   coast, but the RN cruised the region
   while Baratarian pirates, acting on their
   own, also preyed on US ships. These
   efforts destroyed commercial shipping,
   but the USN was not prevented from
   operating against the Spanish and pirates.
3. In 1814–15, the British failed to capture
   New Orleans, which they wanted to use
   as a bargaining point in peace negotiations
   and perhaps use to check American
   territorial ambitions.

fighting devastated the Indigenous population and led survivors either to flee to Spanish territory or to sign away half their territory to the United States. During America's conflicts with the Muscogees, the British made small efforts to provide support to advance their own objectives but connections between them and the southern First Nations were limited.

In the final months of fighting, the British hoped to seize the lower reaches of the Mississippi River to strengthen their position in peace negotiations – or even to affirm Spanish Florida's independence from the United States and perhaps create a new political entity in the lower Mississippi, because the ethnic diversity of the region and the American government's tenuous authority there suggested that boundaries could be redrawn. The first major British act was to send an inadequately small force on a failed expedition to capture Fort Bowyer at Mobile Point in September 1814 in preparation for an assault against New Orleans. The main expedition, however, had to wait until the blistering summer and hurricane seasons ended. After assembling troops in

In a daring 1814 action, British forces captured the US Navy's Lake Borgne squadron in an attack that culminated in violent hand-to-hand fighting. (Oil, 1830s–40s, Everett Collection Inc / Alamy Stock Photo)

Bermuda and the West Indies, the British sailed to New Orleans, arriving near their target in December with 7,500 men.

Anticipating the attack, the American commander, Major-General Andrew Jackson, deployed a flotilla consisting primarily of gunboats to Lake Borgne to guard one of the approaches to New Orleans. The British used small boats to attack and capture it on 14 December. This helped them land near the city with assistance from local Spanish and Portuguese fishermen who held little regard for the American government. However, unexpectedly cold weather, combined with the deep swamps and difficult terrain, created serious supply problems, and contributed to deaths through illness and exposure during the arduous advance on New Orleans. Then, on 23 December, Jackson led a combined naval and land attack against the British camp at the Villeré Plantation outside of the city. With difficulty, the redcoats held their own in the confused night action and the Americans pulled back.

Jackson fortified the approach to New Orleans at the Rodriguez Canal, which he equipped partly with artillery, powder, and shot supplied by the local Baratarian pirates who allied themselves to their erstwhile enemy in the face of the British presence. Meanwhile, the senior officer in the British expedition, Major-General Sir Edward Pakenham, ordered the destruction of a schooner, the *Carolina*, which had participated in the attack on Villeré plantation, with hot shot. On 28 December, he performed a reconnaissance in strength against Jackson's line, but was forced to withdraw, despite coming close to breaking one of the American flanks. Then, on 1 January 1815, he bombarded the Americans, hoping to silence their artillery, but with little effect because the British did not have enough ammunition and because their guns sank into the soggy ground of the lowland environment. American artillery fire did considerable damage in return. A week later, on 8 January, the British made their famous but ill-executed frontal assault against Jackson's line. They carried one

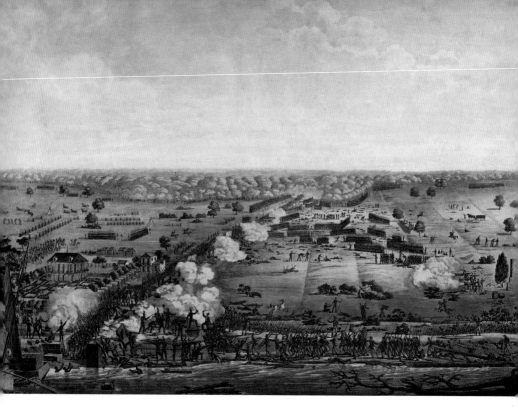

This detailed image of the 1815 battle of New Orleans copies a painting by Louisiana militiaman Jean-Hyacinthe de Laclotte, who participated in the fighting. (Print, c.1818, Everett Collection Inc / Alamy Stock Photo)

of the batteries at bayonet point, but the main attack collapsed into disaster, and Pakenham fell in action. The British withdrew, having experienced their worst defeat in the war, and, like the Americans, having fought the battle without being aware that diplomats had agreed to peace terms two weeks earlier.

Despite heavy losses in their operations against New Orleans, the British made two more attacks against American posts. One, against Fort St Philip near New Orleans, failed in January. The other, against Fort Bowyer, succeeded when its garrison capitulated in February, and which the British took in preparation for a move against Mobile. The next day, however, word of the peace treaty arrived, and the soldiers and sailors shifted their attention to the task of going home.

Propaganda

Both sides used propaganda to advance their cause, boost morale among their people, and win approval on the international stage. One example of this was the reluctance of Americans to speak openly about expansionism as a reason for war, preferring instead to condemn their Indigenous and British enemies for outrages in frontier areas and on the high seas. Similarly, the government in London downplayed maritime tensions and concentrated on issues related to defending their colonies and assisting the First Nations in protecting their homelands. Troops from both armies committed crimes against civilians (although on a small scale compared to other contemporary conflicts), as represented by a number of murders and rapes at the capture of Hampton by former French prisoners-of-war who had been recruited into British service, but each side expressed outrage when their enemy was the perpetrator, and regularly exaggerated the nature of the offences committed. Bald-faced lies formed another element in the propaganda war. After the capture of York in 1813, for example, Americans read broadsides proclaiming that their soldiers had dispersed 1,000 warriors, when in fact there only were 40–60 of them in the battle. (Exaggerations and misinformation continue to pollute modern interpretations of the conflict.)

The murder of about 30 US prisoners by warriors after the 1813 battle of Frenchtown provided Americans with anti-British and racialized anti-Indigenous propaganda opportunities. (Print, 1813, William L. Clements Library, University of Michigan)

Much of the propaganda war focused on the First Nations. US newspapers regularly condemned scalping and the desecration of the dead; yet the reality was that American combatants also were willing to commit indignities upon their enemies, as occurred in 1812 when Brigadier-General Alexander Smyth offered $40 bounties for Indigenous scalps. A year later, an American officer met a Kentuckian who 'had two Indian scalps that he had taken at Frenchtown' and who 'fleshed them with his knife, salted them, and set them in hoops in true Indian style'. American newspapers condemned First Nations enemies for killing prisoners after the battle of Frenchtown on the Raisin River in 1813, which generated the war cry, 'Remember the Raisin' to motivate their troops in the Old Northwest.

However, these same newspapers remained silent about American acts of brutality, such as the murder, scalping, and disfigurement of a captured British soldier and Canadian militiaman later that year, in which the militiaman apparently had not been killed before being butchered. For their part, the tribespeople criticized the dissonance between words and deeds. In 1813, for instance, British officers reprimanded some warriors for mutilating an American corpse on the Niagara Peninsula but an Odawa chief, Blackbird, replied that their enemy had disinterred Indigenous dead and chopped up the bodies, and then declared: 'If the Big Knives when they kill people of our colour leave them without hacking them to pieces, we will follow their example.'

Protest

Many people opposed their leaders' decisions in the War of 1812. Among the First Nations, individuals generally were free to ignore a community decision to engage in hostilities, or at least could determine the extent to which they would support the general consensus. This independence even included being able to desert in the face of enemy fire without serious repercussions beyond negatively affecting their reputations. Within settler society, militia service was not voluntary because eligible men were obliged to assemble when called out (although the regular armies on both sides were composed of volunteers). The ability of the combatant governments to exert their authority, however, was limited enough that those who violated laws, such as militiamen who failed to muster when ordered to do so or who went home while serving when they became dissatisfied, usually did not face any consequences. Some politicians opposed their governments as well, as exemplified in 1812 when the legislative assembly of Upper Canada rejected Isaac Brock's request to suspend some civil liberties in order to allow the army to defend the province more effectively. Prominent individuals on both sides expressed their disagreement with the authorities freely, as seen in New England when the Revd Elijah Parish denounced James Madison for going to war against Britain, which he saw as the bulwark against Napoleonic absolutism, with the words: 'If we engage in this war, then we take the side with the despot; we enlist under his fatal banner ... and must share in his approaching destruction.'

Treason – helping the enemy – of course, could bring the death penalty, but even then, there were far fewer prosecutions than there were incidents. Often, the authorities overlooked cases of assisting the enemy among their populations in occupied territory, as happened when the British army marched on Washington in 1814 and people sold them food, offered to guide the way to the capital, and provided intelligence to the invaders. On the British side, the grisliest event that involved cases of aiding the enemy was the 'Bloody Assize' of May and June 1814. Held in Ancaster on the Niagara Escarpment, a court tried 19 Upper Canadians who had been captured while serving with the Americans. Charged with high treason, one admitted his crime while the court acquitted four men but found 14 to be guilty. After imposing the death sentence, the judges held back the executions for a month to give the men the opportunity to supplicate royal mercy. A number of them were hung; others were banished from the British Empire; and some either escaped to the United States or died of typhus in jail.

For Americans, the most memorable story of potentially disloyal activity was that of the Hartford Convention in December and January 1814–15. Held in the Connecticut capital, it arose from New England's frustrations with the war. Beyond the region's general opposition to the conflict, state officials thought they needed to keep control of their militia regiments despite Washington's attempts to deploy them elsewhere because the federal government's defensive efforts in the region were inadequate. Madison's tax increases angered people,

New England's well-trained militia (despite some eccentric uniforms) usually stayed home largely because of regional opposition to the war. (Artefact, 1810s–20s, © Don Troiani. All Rights Reserved 2023 / Bridgeman Images)

and the British blockade, raids, and occupations created enormous dismay. As the convention met, a number of New England newspapers called for secession from the American union and the signing of a separate peace with Britain. The federal government was so concerned that it sent troops to Hartford in case there was an attempt to take New England out of the republic. The majority of delegates, however, were more moderate than the press, and, despite the misunderstandings of the Madison administration and subsequent popular memory, it was not a seditious enterprise. Its final report did not pose a challenge to the nation, being instead a plea to restore New England's declining powers within the country. As one politician, Josiah Quincy, noted when asked what he thought its outcome would be, the worst consequence he could imagine was publication of 'a great pamphlet!'

Civilian populations

As in most wars, civilians suffered as the fighting raged around them, whether they were British, Canadian, Indigenous, or American, as noted earlier. Among the many other problems they faced, inflation made life difficult and militia service took people away from jobs they needed to fulfil in order to support their families. British taxpayers demanded relief after enduring substantial burdens in the long period of war between 1793 and 1815. Some people had to give up property for military use, as shipowners did when the opposing forces acquired their vessels to enlarge their squadrons on the freshwater lakes along the Canadian-American border. After battles, civilians chose to, or had to, open their homes to the wounded, while soldiers and camp followers robbed the dead, and lawless locals exploited the chaos to loot their neighbours. Homes were robbed and burned, often by troops disregarding orders to respect property – and on occasion these deeds were committed by men ostensibly fighting to protect

The village of Queenston on the Niagara River was one of the Canadian, Indigenous, and American civilian communities destroyed or devastated during the war. (Print, 1814, McCord Stewart Museum, Gift of David Ross McCord)

them. Sometimes soldiers, militiamen, or warriors assaulted, tortured, or murdered civilians across the war's different theatres. Regularly people had to abandon their property and flee from the fighting to seek shelter as refugees far from their homes, often in exposed conditions in inclement weather, as occurred on both sides of the Niagara River in the winter of 1813–14. Naturally, many died because of the traumas they endured. Others, however, profited from the war by feeding, transporting, clothing, equipping, housing, and entertaining combatants. In the case of the latter, one British army surgeon noted that he treated venereal disease so often in comparison to battlefield wounds that he mused that the army's camp followers posed a greater threat to Canadian security than the American army did. Even selling goods and services to the enemy proved to be profitable, as New York and New England farmers found in looking for markets for their produce.

Soldiers' families often travelled with their menfolk, living through the same privations on campaign as

Military families often endured hard lives, as Thomas Rowlandson's representation of a soldier's widow attempts to capture in this interpretation. (Watercolour, 1815–20, Courtesy National Gallery of Art, Washington/ John F. McCrindle Collection, CC0)

they did, and occasionally found themselves left behind enemy lines, as some of those associated with the British army did after the fall of Fort George in 1813. Civilian seamen endured indignities, captivity, wounds, and death at the hands of enemy navies and privateers, and American sailors held captive in England waited months in grim conditions once the war ended before authorities could arrange their release and repatriation. People also grieved lost loved ones who had died while on military service. Others found their existence constrained or impoverished after the war because they needed to care for

the broken bodies and minds of their veteran relatives who otherwise would have been expected to contribute to the family's well-being if they had survived in good health. Governments and charities provided help, as did generous individuals who were moved by the plight of those in need, but relief rarely was equal to demand. The Loyal and Patriotic Society of Upper Canada, for instance, gave widows and orphans £25 to help those who lost husbands or fathers, but that amount would last only a short while. Naturally, for those who had experienced privation or violence at the hands of the enemy, the war created long-term feelings of hostility, and thereby helped to strengthen patriotic sentiment or nurtured it where it did not exist before, such as among American immigrants in Canada who turned against their former homeland (and whose service in the militia had been better than most observers had predicted it would be when the war broke out).

The 1824 Brock monument on the Queenston Heights battlefield symbolized an anti-American identity engendered in Canada because of the US invasions of 1812–14. (Oil, 1830, Icom Images / Alamy Stock Photo)

HOW THE WAR ENDED
The peace of Christmas Eve

The Treaty of Ghent

Efforts to prevent, and then end, the conflict began at the time it broke out, starting with the British revocation of the orders-in-council before the king's government knew that hostilities had started. This was followed by a suggestion from the American chargé d'affairs in London that Britain should renounce impressment in return for an armistice, but Lord Liverpool and his cabinet were unwilling to concede on that issue. Shortly afterwards, when the British captured Detroit, and news of the repeal of the orders reached Canada and the United States, Sir George Prevost arranged an armistice for the eastern part of the Great Lakes region with the local American commander to enable the government in Washington to reconsider its plans. However, James Madison, with his country's army humiliated in the war's first encounters, decided to continue the war to conquer Canada, suppress the Indigenous peoples, end impressment, and achieve his trade and other goals.

In March 1813, Russia offered to mediate a peace, but Lord Liverpool did not trust the tsar's government. Instead, he wanted British diplomats to negotiate directly with their American counterparts. In January 1814, the two belligerents agreed to meet in Ghent (in modern Belgium), after having rejected another choice, the Swedish city of Gothenburg, once European affairs progressed far enough in favour of Britain to make it safe to assemble in the more convenient location. Representatives of the two countries first met there in August.

Naturally, both sides tried to gain as many concessions as possible, expanding or restraining their demands in relation to the evolving situation in Europe and the successes or failures of their respective militaries in North America. The fundamental difference between the two, however, revolved around Britain's objectives to retain both Canada and the means London used

Lieutenant-General Sir George Prevost successfully managed the defence of British North America. Nevertheless, his reputation collapsed due to his failure to capture Plattsburgh in 1814. (Oil, 1808–15, McCord Stewart Museum, Gift of David Ross McCord)

to protect its maritime interests. Opportunistically, the British thought it also might be possible to use America's poor military performance to force the United States to accept the creation of an Indigenous homeland in the Old Northwest, make changes along the Canadian border to improve colonial defence, and gain other advantages. In contrast, Washington wanted to change Britain's naval practices and annex at least part of Canada if it could not get all the North American colonies. Its secondary desires included demands for compensation for damage to property and the loss of several thousand slaves who had fled to the British when they raided the country's saltwater coasts, along with preserving pre-war rights, such as access to British North American fisheries. Beyond these, the Madison administration hoped to cripple the ability of Britain's First Nations allies within the republic's borders to resist settler expansion onto their territories, and to use diplomatic gains it might make against Britain to advance expansionary desires against Spain.

Given that the United States was the stronger power in North America, Lord Liverpool worried that the retention of Canada might be endangered if the war were to continue into 1815, despite the American military failures and the financial and other challenges the republic faced. At the same time, the fragile peace in Europe showed signs of disintegration as the diplomats argued over terms, which meant that the troops recently sent west across the Atlantic needed to sail back. Therefore, he put opportunistic demands aside to focus on securing Britain's primary goals. Meanwhile, the Americans realized that they could not achieve any of their objectives, either primary or secondary. Furthermore, the United States government faced bankruptcy, recruitment for the army fell below the rate at which men were being lost, and federal officials did not realize that the secessionist movement in New England was weak. Consequently, the American delegates thought the best they could get was the preservation of the status quo that they had been fighting

Both sides benefited from free and enslaved Black service, including slaves in British West Indian regiments who gained freedom after their enlistment period. (Oil, c.1803, © National Army Museum / Bridgeman Images)

to upset, especially as conquest was proving impossible (and the British actually controlled larger quantities of US territory in 1814 than the Americans occupied in Canada). Thus, both parties agreed to a treaty based on the principal of 'status quo ante bellum' – the return of everything to pre-war conditions, including the return of captured territory.

The treaty likewise required both sides to make peace with the First Nations who fought against them and to restore the rights they had enjoyed in 1811. This was a more significant concession for the United States than for Great Britain because of the Indigenous situation on America's borderlands. The two powers also set aside several issues for resolution in the future. These included an agreement to conduct a survey of the Canadian-American border to determine the exact boundary line defined in the 1783 Treaty of Paris that had recognized the independence of the former Thirteen Colonies, as both sides acknowledged that their assumptions were not necessarily correct. (The survey made small adjustments to fulfil the intent of the 1783 treaty, although some people have claimed – incorrectly – that those minor alterations, like the transfer of Drummond and Carleton islands to the United States, represented wartime conquests.) In another post-war decision, Americans lost part of their access to Canadian fisheries that they had enjoyed before 1812. The only change from the status quo in the Treaty of Ghent itself was an American agreement to assist the British in suppressing the Atlantic slave trade. On 24 December, the diplomats signed the peace treaty and then celebrated the coming of Christmas in Ghent cathedral.

On 30 December 1814, the British Parliament approved the treaty. Across the Atlantic, the US Senate unanimously ratified the treaty on 16 February 1815, bringing the war to its official end. Much of eastern North America heard the news within about two weeks, although isolated posts on the Mississippi did not learn about the return of peace until the spring. The good news took longer to reach distant corners of the world, and so, far away, between the Java Sea and the Indian Ocean in June 1815, the USS *Peacock* fired upon the East India Company brig *Nautilus*, killing and wounding 14 people, despite the fact that its officers told the sceptical Americans that the war had ended.

After three years of hostility, people moved quickly to re-establish their normal lives. Within two days of negotiations concluding in Ghent, London business interests learned enough to begin adapting their investments to take advantage of renewed trade with the United States. Later, the RN commander in Upper Canada, Sir James Lucas Yeo, accepted an invitation from his former rival, Commodore Isaac Chauncey, to visit Sackett's Harbour with his fellow officers, who, in their hurry to get back to England, took the faster route home via New York City rather than through Quebec. With the coming of spring, both sides withdrew their forces from occupied territories and began to send prisoners home. Within the Indigenous world, negotiations took place through 1815, 1816, and 1817 to end the fighting between the First Nations that already had not arranged peace agreements with their enemies, whether they were the white powers or other tribes.

Perceptions of victory

As word spread west across the Atlantic that peace had returned, people felt relief as the war's burdens and uncertainties lifted and as most in contested regions could look to a future with greater optimism. The majority of Americans forgot why their country went to war and the failure of their soldiers, sailors, and diplomats to achieve their government's objectives. Instead, they embraced the memories of success at Plattsburgh, Baltimore, and especially New Orleans, to bolster an interpretation of the peace that affirmed the power and dignity of their country, even proclaiming that they won a second war of independence despite the fact that independence never was threatened. Some pronounced their enthusiasm for the outcome with breathtaking exaggeration: Congressman George Troup, for one, declared that the Treaty of Ghent was 'the glorious termination of the most glorious war ever waged by any people'.

As time passed, the legends of American victory grew. In 1816, the famous Democratic-Republican newspaper *Niles Register* crowed: 'we did virtually dictate the Treaty of Ghent to the British', ignoring the fact that getting the status quo of 1811 restored was difficult enough, while vague and meaningless affirmations that Britain emerged from the war with a newfound respect for the United States helped to solidify such views. As far as Americans remember the war today, such attitudes dominate the public consciousness, as can be seen in popular publications, textbooks, the media, and some academic writing. Other Americans in 1815 saw things differently, with the Federalists who opposed the Madison administration noting how his government had failed to accomplish its goals. That view, less helpful in building national identity and patriotism, has been embraced by fewer Americans, both then and through subsequent decades, but does enjoy some standing, particularly in scholarly literature. Another common idea that has survived to the present is the assertion that the war was a draw since it did not change anything – but that perspective overlooks the fact that not changing anything was the main British objective.

An assessment of goals set by the two powers in 1812 and realized in 1815 points to British success. The United Kingdom achieved its primary war aims and the United States did not. On maritime issues, the government in London understood that the country's pre-war policies risked conflict with the Americans but believed that it could not renounce all of them because of the imperative to defeat the French and save the British Isles and the broader European continent from their hostile plans. Yet, as the possibility of conflict with America grew through the early months of 1812, it rescinded the orders-in-council to avoid a confrontation before learning about Washington's decision to go to war, so the revocation had nothing to do with the conflict itself. Britain would not negotiate a compromise on impressment or other maritime policies, and so the peace treaty was silent on these matters. These issues evaporated as Anglo-American problems because of Britain's triumph over France, not because of US actions. In fact, London came out of the war fully prepared to implement similar restrictions should future tensions require them, as the government would when it blockaded Germany in 1914 despite Washington's objections.

Crucially, Britain defended its colonies successfully. Thus, the Canadian experiment in building a distinct North American society was not brought to a violent and premature close through conquest, but continued, as it does today. This was the most significant outcome of the

War of 1812. Additionally, the retention of these colonies (and their subsequent identity as a nation within British Empire and Commonwealth) gave the United Kingdom secure access to North American products outside of the control of the United States and contributed to the overall strength of the Empire. It also provided the mother country with vital support in 1914 and 1939 when Canada went to war, while the Americans stayed out of the great conflicts of the 20th century until 1917 and 1941.

While the case for a fundamental British success over the United States is the most logical one that can be made in relation to the historical evidence, there were participants in the conflict whose stories differ. Although their fights had only peripheral connections to the Anglo-American war, the resistance to US expansion in the Spanish colonies and the Muscogee confederacy in the south failed. More closely related to the conflict between Great Britain and the United States were the semi-distinct wars of the First Nations in the north and west, who, aside from neutralists, divided into Canadian-resident tribespeople who generally (if conditionally) supported the British, American-resident peoples who allied with the Madison administration, and those who lived within the borders of the republic who fought against it. This last group was the largest and potentially the most vulnerable. The Treaty of Ghent restored their pre-existing territorial and other rights, but this was far less than the independent homeland that the majority of tribespeople on the American frontier wanted. However, the one campaign that US forces won on the Canadian front was in the Detroit region, which led a sizeable number of the Indigenous communities in the Old Northwest to make peace with the United States before the end of the Anglo-American war. This made it difficult for British diplomats to argue for a homeland for them without a corresponding willingness to continue fighting into 1815 to achieve that goal. Doing so was not in the interests of either the United Kingdom or its Canadian colonies because the Americans might win battles and change the strategic situation, so that part of British North America might have been lost.

William Henry
Harrison was a
great enemy of
Indigenous people,
alienating land
through aggressive
treaties and fighting
them successfully in
the Old Northwest
and Canada. (Oil,
c.1813, photo
by Heritage Art/
Heritage Images via
Getty Images)

Nevertheless, the article that restored Indigenous rights to their 1811 status was not insubstantial. The problem was that it did not preclude the United States from working to alienate First Nations lands and reduce their rights after having restored them. Tragically, communities that allied with the Americans, such as the Haudenosaunee in New York, received no better treatment from the republic's government and citizens after 1815 than those who fought against them. Indigenous people in Canada similarly suffered as settlement pressures accelerated following the war and as newcomers wanted their land, although the loss of territory occurred at a slower pace and without the degree of military violence that marked the experience of the tribes south of the border. Nevertheless, it created hardships and legacies that continue to afflict relations between the First Nations and Canada today, similar to the problems faced by Indigenous people in the United States.

A permanent peace?

The end of the War of 1812 brought permanent peace between Great Britain and the United States, and politicians at cross-boundary events in North America today like to speak about the world's longest undefended border, claiming that it has existed for over 200 years. The reality is more complex. Military planners did not know that peace would last, so they prepared for a future conflict. Both sides agreed that a major reason for the US failure to conquer Upper Canada was its inability to sever the St Lawrence supply line by capturing either Kingston or Montreal. Consequently, the two powers strengthened fortifications and communications lines with a focus on that region. The greatest of those projects was the Rideau Canal, built by the British between 1826 and 1832 as an alternative water route between the Ottawa River at Bytown (now Ottawa) and Kingston in place of the vulnerable St Lawrence, which would help them keep supply lines open to the upper province in the event of renewed hostilities. Among other works, they built a citadel in Kingston in the 1830s and added several Martello towers around the town in the 1840s to protect their main Lake Ontario naval base. The Americans likewise improved their fortifications and built roads to facilitate a possible future invasion. Farther west, they

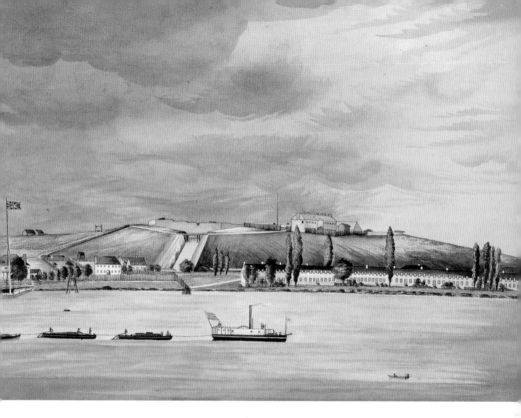

worked to cut the ties between the British in Canada and the tribes of the Old Northwest and upper Mississippi. In part, British and American efforts were little more than prudent planning rather than serious preparations for conflict, but both powers thought of the other as a prospective enemy through the decades that followed the Treaty of Ghent.

Nevertheless, neither government wanted war, and each hoped to avoid unnecessary military spending. Therefore, in 1816–17, the British minister to Washington, Sir Charles Bagot, and the acting US secretary of state, Richard Rush, negotiated a plan for naval disarmament on the Canadian-American border. Accepted in 1817, the Rush–Bagot Agreement limited each side to a small number of armed vessels across the Great Lakes and on Lake Champlain. Most of the 1812-era warships were put in 'ordinary' for future use until they rotted away, or were sunk, broken up, or sold to civilians. (Nevertheless, both sides violated the

Fort Henry was one of the British army's major post-war construction projects. It guarded Kingston, its naval dockyard, and the Rideau Canal's southern entrance. (Watercolour, 1839, Library and Archives Canada)

agreement during periods of tension between the two powers.) When potentially threatening problems arose, as occurred in the 1830s, 1840s, 1860s, and 1890s, the two powers nevertheless maintained peace, despite such challenges as periodic demands for the annexation of Canada from influential American politicians and others. In 1917, over a century after the end of the War of 1812, the United States joined the great struggle against Germany and its allies, and international cooperation among Britons, Canadians, and Americans dominated much of the history of the century that followed.

Legacies

The War of 1812 was a small conflict compared with the great Napoleonic struggles that were its contemporaries and that contributed to its genesis. The Duke of Wellington, for instance, commanded more men at the battle of Waterloo outside Brussels in 1815 than the maximum number of British soldiers deployed across

Re-enactors – such as these at Fort Erie – contribute to studying and commemorating the war, along with historians, heritage site and museum personnel, and others. (Cosmo Condina North America / Alamy Stock Photo)

all of North America at the height of the War of 1812. This has meant that the British generally have forgotten the conflict. In the United States, memories survive, but mainly have been subsumed by those of the successful war with Mexico in 1846–48, in which the US expanded into Texas, California, and neighbouring regions due partly to a military establishment that improved in light of the lessons learned between 1812 and 1815. Afterwards, the great national crisis of the Civil War of 1861–65 shook Americans, eclipsing the conflicts with Britain and Mexico in the public consciousness. In Canada, the War of 1812 was the gravest threat to its security in the 19th century; therefore, it has occupied a larger place in the country's historical memory than it has in either of the other two countries.

The war continues to attract attention. It has a place in the standard histories of the United States and Canada. It also remains alive in the memories of First Nations communities whose ancestors played vital roles in the conflict. Beyond these generalities, there are communities of people today interested in the war, ranging from academic historians to armchair enthusiasts,

While the president's mansion was whitewashed after the British burned it, the name 'White House' predates the war, and refers to its whitish stone construction. (Print, 1814, Library of Congress)

to re-enactors who bring the conflict to life, to the staff and volunteers who manage and preserve historic sites and museums associated with the events of 1812–15. Federal, state, provincial, and local governments, along with non-profit organizations, maintain monuments and plaques across eastern North America to commemorate a wide range of themes related to the war. Small numbers of monuments may be found in the United Kingdom as well. St Paul's Cathedral in London, for example, houses memorials to a number of the war's leading British combatants. Sometimes the conflict has been described as a forgotten war, but if one looks, there are reminders to be found in many places. This is as it should be because of its significance in the history of North America (and beyond), despite being a relatively small struggle in comparison to both its Napoleonic contemporaries and to others that occurred in the continent's past during different periods.

This allegory of peace by an Englishman living in America captures the relief felt by many when news of the Treaty of Ghent became known. (Print, c.1815, Library of Congress)

CHRONOLOGY

Land, freshwater, and coastal war:
AC = Atlantic Coast; GC = Gulf Coast; GL = Great Lakes;
UM = Upper Mississippi

Saltwater war:
AO = Atlantic Ocean, Caribbean Sea, and connected waterways;
IO = Indian Ocean; PO = Pacific Ocean

* Indicated that at least 5 per cent of the participants in a battle or other violent confrontation were Indigenous on one or both sides (while at some, their participation on one side could be as high as 100 per cent)

Small military confrontations are not included

1783	Treaty of Paris acknowledges the independence of the United States from Great Britain
1786–95	American-Indigenous conflict occurs in the Ohio country*
1793–1815	Anglo-French war takes place (except briefly in 1802–03, 1814)
1798–1801	Quasi-War occurs between France and US
1805	Tecumseh and Tenskwatawa begin to form the Western Tribal Confederacy
1805–11	British orders-in-councils, impressment, blockades, and other actions negatively affect US relations
1806–11	French decrees and other measures adversely distress American commerce
1806–11	US responds to British and French restrictions with laws and other efforts
1807	HMS *Leopard* fires on USS *Chesapeake*; removes deserters from RN
1811	USS *President* attacks HMS *Little Belt*
1811	Americans repulse the Western Tribes at Tippecanoe; burn Prophetstown*
1811	US Congress begins to debate war with Great Britain

1812

04 Apr US, anticipating war, adopts embargo to save ships from seizure: AO

18 Jun US goes to go to war against Great Britain

23 Jun Britain repeals orders-in-council, unaware that war began

12 Jul Americans invade Canada from Detroit; skirmish with British: GL*

16 Jul USS *Nautilus* surrenders to a Royal Navy squadron: AO

17 Jul Americans surrender Fort Mackinac: GL*

05 Aug British defeat Americans at Brownstown: GL*

07–11 Aug Americans withdraw from Canada to Detroit: GL

09 Aug Americans fail to open communications at Maguaga: GL*

13 Aug USS *Essex* captures HMS *Alert*: AO

15 Aug Americans suffer defeat outside Fort Dearborn: GL*

16 Aug Americans surrender Detroit, north-west army, and Michigan: GL*

19 Aug USS *Constitution* defeats, then burns HMS *Guerrière*: AO

04–15 Sep Americans repel Indigenous forces at Forts Harrison and Wayne: GL*

05–08 Sep Americans defend Fort Madison against Indigenous attack: UM*

Oct RN begins a limited blockade of the US: AC

09 Oct Americans capture HMS *Caledonia* and *Detroit*; burn *Detroit*: GL

13 Oct British defeat Americans at Queenston Heights: GL*

18 Oct USS *Wasp* captures HMS *Frolic*: AO

18 Oct HMS *Poictiers* captures USS *Wasp* (and *Frolic*): AO

25 Oct USS *United States* captures HMS *Macedonian*: AO

20 Nov American thrust against Montreal collapses at Lacolle: GL*

22 Nov HMS *Southampton* captures USS *Vixen*: AO

28 Nov British repulse Americans at Frenchman's Creek: GL*

17–18 Dec Americans destroy Mississinewa Indigenous villages: GL*

29 Dec USS *Constitution* defeats, then burns HMS *Java*: AO

1813

Jan RN begins a formal blockade of Chesapeake and Delaware rivers: AC

17 Jan HMS *Narcissus* captures USS *Viper*: AO

22 Jan British defeat Americans at Frenchtown: GL*

Feb RN extends blockade between the Delaware and Chesapeake: AC

Feb British begin raiding US coast: AC

22 Feb British defeat Americans at Ogdensburg: GL

24 Feb USS *Hornet* sinks HMS *Peacock*: AO

Mar RN extends blockade north to New York, south to Georgia: AC

27 Apr Americans capture York: GL*

28 Apr–09 May Americans defend Fort Meigs (first siege): GL*

03 May British defeat Americans at Havre de Grace: AC

27 May Americans capture Fort George; British then abandon nearby posts: GL*

29 May Americans defend Sackett's Harbour: GL

01 Jun HMS *Shannon* captures USS *Chesapeake*: AO

03 Jun British capture USS *Growler* and *Eagle* near the north end of Lake Champlain: GL

06 Jun British defeat Americans at Stoney Creek: GL

08 Jun British attack Americans at Forty Mile Creek; American withdraw to Fort George; British afterwards reoccupy previously abandoned posts: GL*

22 Jun Americans defend Craney Island: AC

24 Jun Americans suffer defeat at Beaver Dams: GL*

25 Jun British defeat Americans at Hampton: AC

28 Jun–09 Oct British blockade Americans in Fort George: GL*

11 Jul British destroy American depot at Black Rock: GL*

21–28 Jul Americans defend Fort Meigs (second siege): GL*

29 Jul British repulse Americans at Burlington Beach: GL

31 Jul–03 Aug British destroy American facilities around Plattsburgh: GL

01–02 Aug Americans defend Fort Stephenson: GL*
05 Aug British seize Kent Island: AC
08–10 Aug USN loses two vessels capsized and two captured on Lake Ontario: GL
14 Aug HMS *Pelican* captures USS *Argus*: AO
05 Sep USS *Enterprise* captures HMS *Boxer*: AO
10 Sep USN squadron captures RN squadron on Lake Erie: GL
18 Sep British evacuate Detroit region: GL
05 Oct Americans defeat British at Moraviantown; many in the Western Tribes later negotiate peace with US: GL*
26 Oct British defeat Americans at Châteauguay: GL*
Nov RN extends blockade from New York to Narragansett Bay: AC
Nov Americans burn Peoria and neighbouring Indigenous villages: UM*
04 Nov Americans evacuate and burn Fort Madison after Indigenous harassment: UM*
11 Nov British defeat Americans at Crysler's Farm: GL
10–11 Dec Americans evacuate Fort George; destroy Niagara and Queenston: GL
12 Dec British reoccupy Fort George: GL
19 Dec British capture Fort Niagara: GL
19–30 Dec British burn Lewiston, Tuscarora, Fort Schlosser, Black Rock, and Buffalo: GL*
25 Dec HMS *Belvidera* captures USS *Vixen* II: AO

1814

16–24 Jan British destroy American resources in NY's Franklin County area: GL
14 Feb USS *Constitution* captures and destroys HMS *Pictou*: AO
04 Mar Americans defeat British at Longwoods: GL*
28 Mar HMS *Phoebe* and *Cherub* capture USS *Essex* and *Essex Junior*: PO
30 Mar British defeat Americans at Lacolle: GL*
06 Apr Napoleon abdicates; British resources gradually freed for the American war
07–08 Apr British raid Pettipaug (Essex): AC
20 Apr HMS *Orpheus* and *Shelburne* capture USS *Frolic*: AO
28 Apr USS *Peacock* captures HMS *Epervier*: AO

May RN extends blockade to New England: AC
06 May British capture Oswego: GL
14–15 May Americans raid Port Dover and region: GL*
30 May Americans defeat British at Sandy Creek: GL*
02 Jun Americans occupy Prairie du Chien: UM*
22 Jun HMS *Leander* captures USS *Rattlesnake*: AO
28 Jun USS *Wasp* II captures and burns HMS *Reindeer*:
AO
03 Jul Americans capture Fort Erie: GL
05 Jul Americans defeat British at Chippawa: GL*
11–12 Jul Americans surrender Fort Sullivan; British
occupy Eastport: AC
12 Jul HMS *Medway* captures USS *Syren*: AO
20 Jul Americans surrender Prairie du Chien/Fort Shelby:
UM*
21 Jul Americans suffer defeat at Campbell's Island: UM*
25 Jul Americans lose the initiative on the Niagara River
at Lundy's Lane: GL
03 Aug Americans repulse British at Conjocta Creek: GL
03 Aug–21 Sep Americans defend Fort Erie: GL
04 Aug British repulse Americans on Mackinac Island:
GL*
08 Aug Peace negotiations begin in Ghent
12 Aug British capture USS *Somers* and *Ohio* on Lake
Erie: GL
14 Aug Americans destroy HMS *Nancy* and a depot on
Georgian Bay: GL*
22 Aug Americans destroy their flotilla to prevent capture
near Pig Point: AC
24 Aug British defeat Americans at Bladensburg; capture
Washington; Americans burn their navy yard and ships:
AC
27–29 Aug Americans withdraw from, and blow up, Fort
Washington; British occupy Alexandria: AC
01 Sep British occupy Castine and Belfast: AC
01 Sep USS *Wasp* II sinks HMS *Avon*: AO
03 Sep British seize Hampden: AC
03–06 Sep British capture USS *Tigress* and *Scorpion* on
Lake Huron: GL*
05 Sep British occupy Bangor: AC

05 Sep Americans suffer defeat at Credit Island: UM*
10–11 Sep British capture Fort O'Brien; occupy Machias: AC
11 Sep American squadron defeats British squadron on Lake Champlain: GL
12 Sep British defeat Americans at North Point: AC
13–14 Sep Americans withstand bombardment of Forts Covington and McHenry; save Baltimore: AC
14–16 Sep Americans defend Fort Bowyer (first attack): GC*
19 Oct Americans repulse British at Cook's Mill: GL
25 Oct–17 Nov Americans raid Lake Erie region (McArthur's Raid): GL*
05 Nov Americans evacuate and blow up Fort Erie; retire to Buffalo: GL
14 Dec British capture American Lake Borgne squadron: GC
15 Dec–05 Jan Hartford Convention occurs
23 Dec Americans fail to drive British from Villeré Plantation: GC
24 Dec Peace negotiations conclude in Ghent
30 Dec British Parliament approves the Treaty of Ghent

1815   **08 Jan** Americans defeat British at New Orleans after unsuccessful British probes on 28 Dec and 01 Jan: GC
09–18 Jan Americans defend Fort St Philip: GC
15 Jan RN squadron captures USS *President*: AO
12 Feb Americans surrender Fort Bowyer (second attack): GC
16 Feb War ends with the US ratification of the Treaty of Ghent
20 Feb USS *Constitution* captures HMS *Levant* and *Cyane*: AO
11 Mar RN squadron recaptures HMS *Levant*: AO
23 Mar USS *Hornet* captures HMS *Penguin*: AO
30 Jun USS *Peacock* captures East India Company brig *Nautilus*: IO

1815–17   First Nations still at war negotiate peace with their adversaries

FURTHER READING

Primary Sources

Benn, Carl, ed. *Warriors: Native Memoirs from the War of 1812*. Johns Hopkins UP, Baltimore (2014).

—, ed. *A Mohawk Memoir from the War of 1812: John Norton – Teyoninhokarawen*. U of Toronto P, Toronto (2019).

Brannan, John, ed. *Official Letters of the Military and Naval Officers of the United States During the War with Great Britain*. Way and Gideon, Washington (1823).

Cruikshank, Ernest, ed. *The Documentary History of the Campaigns on the Niagara Frontier, 1812–14*. 9 vols. Lundy's Lane Historical Society, Niagara (1902–08).

Dudley, William, & Crawford, Michael, eds. *The Naval War of 1812: A Documentary History*. 3 vols. Naval Historical Center, Washington (1985–2002).

Graves, Donald, ed. *First Campaign of an ADC: The War of 1812 Memoir of Lt William Jenkins Worth, US Army*. (1833–35.) Old Fort Niagara Association, Youngstown (2012).

—, ed. *Merry Hearts Make Light Days: The War of 1812 Journal of Lieutenant John Le Couteur, 104th Foot*. (1993). Robin Brass, Montreal (2012).

Hickey, Donald, ed. *The War of 1812: Writings from America's Second War of Independence*. Library of America, New York (2013).

Memorial of the Inhabitants of Buffalo. Jonathan Elliot, Washington (1817).

Wood, William, ed. *Select British Documents of the Canadian War of 1812*. 4 vols. Champlain Society, Toronto (1920–28).

Secondary Sources

Antal, Sandy. *A Wampum Denied: Procter's War of 1812*. Rev. ed. McGill-Queen's UP, Montreal and Kingston (2011).

Arthur, Brian. *How Britain Won the War of 1812: The Royal Navy's Blockades of the United States, 1812–15*. Boydell & Brewer, Rochester (2011).

Barbuto, Richard. *New York's War of 1812: Politics, Society, and Combat*. U of Oklahoma P, Norman (2021).

Benn, Carl. *Historic Fort York, 1793–1993*. Natural Heritage (Dundurn), Toronto (1993).

—. *The Iroquois in the War of 1812*. U of Toronto P, Toronto (1998).

Braud, Kathryn, ed. *Tohopeka: Rethinking the Creek War and the War of 1812*. U of Alabama P, Tuscaloosa (2012).

Chartrand, René. *A Most Warlike Appearance: Uniforms, Flags, and Equipment of the United States in the War of 1812*. (1992.) Service Publications, Ottawa (2011).

— & Embleton, Gerry. *British Forces in North America, 1793–1815*. Osprey, Oxford (1998).

— & Spedaliere, Donato. *Forts of the War of 1812*. Osprey, Oxford (2012).

Collins, Gilbert. *Guidebook to the Historic Sites of the War of 1812*. Rev. ed. Dundurn, Toronto (2006).

Cusick, James. *The Other War of 1812: The Patriot War and the American Invasion of Spanish East Florida*. UP of Florida, Gainesville (2003).

Dudley, William. *Inside the US Navy of 1812–15*. U of Kansas P, Lawrence (2021).

Edmunds, R. David. *Tecumseh and the Quest for Indian Leadership*. (1984). Pearson Longman, New York (2007).

Elliott, James. *Strange Fatality: The Battle of Stoney Creek, 1813*. Robin Brass, Montreal (2009).

Eustace, Nicole. *1812: War and the Passions of Patriotism*. U of Pennsylvania P, Philadelphia (2012).

Everest, Allan. *The War of 1812 in the Champlain Valley*. (1981). Syracuse UP, Syracuse (2010).

Ferguson, Gillum. *Illinois in the War of 1812*. U of Illinois P, Champaign (2012).

Graves, Dianne. *In the Midst of Alarms: The Untold Story of Women and the War of 1812*. Robin Brass, Montreal (2007).

Graves Donald. 'The Forgotten Soldiers Trilogy': *Field of Glory: The Battle of Crysler's Farm, 1813*; *Where Right and Glory Lead! The Battle of Lundy's Lane, 1814*; & *And All Their Glory Past: Fort Erie, Plattsburgh, and the Final Battles of the North, 1814*. Robin Brass, Montreal (1999–2014).

Grodzinski, John [Tanya]. *Defender of Canada: Sir George Prevost and the War of 1812*. U of Oklahoma P, Norman (2013).

Hickey, Donald. *Don't Give Up the Ship! Myths of the War of 1812*. U of Illinois P, Champaign (2007).

—. *The War of 1812: A Forgotten Conflict*. Rev. ed. U of Illinois P, Champaign (2012).

— & Clark, Connie, eds. *Routledge Handbook of the War of 1812*. Routledge, New York (2016).

Hitsman, J.M. *The Incredible War of 1812*. Rev. by Donald Graves. Robin Brass, Toronto (1999).

Jortner, Adam. *The Gods of Prophetstown: The Battle of Tippecanoe and the Holy War for the American Frontier*. Oxford UP, New York (2011).

Kert, Faye. *Privateering: Patriots and Profits in the War of 1812*. Johns Hopkins UP, Baltimore (2015).

Lambert, Andrew. *The Challenge: Britain Against America in the Naval War of 1812*. Faber and Faber, London (2012).

Lépine, Luc. *Le Québec et la guerre de 1812.* P de l'U Laval, Quebec (2012).

Lord, Walter. *The Dawn's Early Light.* (1972). Johns Hopkins UP, Baltimore (2012).

Malcomson, Robert. *Lords of the Lakes: The Naval War on Lake Ontario 1812–14.* Robin Brass, Montreal (2001).

—. *A Very Brilliant Affair: The Battle of Queenston Heights.* Robin Brass, Montreal (2003).

Reilly, Robin. *The British at the Gates: The New Orleans Campaign in the War of 1812.* Rev. ed. Robin Brass, Montreal (2010).

Shomette, Donald. *Flotilla: The Patuxent Naval Campaign in the War of 1812.* Rev. ed. Johns Hopkins UP, Baltimore (2009).

Skaggs, David. *William Henry Harrison and the Conquest of the Ohio Country.* Johns Hopkins UP, Baltimore (2014).

— & Altoff, Gerard. *A Signal Victory: The Lake Erie Campaign 1812–13.* Rev. ed. Naval Institute, Annapolis (2012).

Smith, Gene. *The Slaves' Gamble: Choosing Sides in the War of 1812.* Palgrave MacMillan, New York (2013).

Stagg, John. *Mr Madison's War: Politics, Diplomacy, and Warfare in the Early American Republic 1783–1830.* Princeton UP, Princeton (1983).

Stoltz, Joseph. *Bloodless Victory: The Battle of New Orleans in History and Memory.* Johns Hopkins UP (2017).

Sugden, John. *Tecumseh: A Life.* Henry Holt, New York (1999).

Whitehorne, Joseph. *The Battle of Baltimore.* Nautical and Aviation Publishing, Baltimore (1997).

Wilder, Patrick. *The Battle of Sackett's Harbour.* Nautical and Aviation Publishing, Baltimore (1994).

Willig, Timothy. *Restoring the Chain of Friendship: British Policy and the Indians of the Great Lakes, 1783–1815.* U of Nebraska P, Lincoln (2008).

Young, George. *The British Capture and Occupation of Downeast Maine.* Penobscot Books, Stonington (2014).

Zaslow, Morris, ed. *The Defended Border: Upper Canada and the War of 1812.* MacMillan, Toronto (1964).

Internet Sources

The list above alerts readers to some of the war's major texts and key themes, while their bibliographies and online catalogues at major libraries provide guidance to other works. Many primary publications and copyright-free secondary works may be consulted via the Internet Archive, Canadiana.org, and similar sites. Academic articles may be examined through databases like 'JSTOR' and 'America History and Life' (although they usually need to be consulted through a subscribing library). There are numerous online reference sources, including the *Dictionary of Canadian Biography* (freely available) and the *American National Biography* (accessible via library subscription). For any of these sources, use discernment, because a sizeable percentage of War of 1812 scholarship is disappointingly weak or immaturely patriotic.

'America's Historic Newspapers', another subscription database, provides searchable opportunities to explore the war in the period's press (which, of course, tends to be biased). Similar databases exist for British periodicals. Some archives make primary manuscripts available online, such as Library and Archives Canada, which presents War of 1812 documents from its microfilm collection. The Internet naturally offers tremendous quantities of 'born digital' material – again requiring caution to avoid bad and out-of-date history. Two under-appreciated sources are the *War of 1812 Magazine* from the Napoleonic Series, presenting articles from a number of the war's leading historians between 2006 and 2018, and the Friends of Fort York *Fife and Drum*, which began publishing excellent articles in 1996. Historic sites, museums, and heritage organizations often provide useful information at their websites. Care should be taken with catalogue information on images and artefacts, however, because errors – such as incorrect dates – are common.

ACKNOWLEDGEMENTS

Thanks are due to historians James Cheevers, Brian Dunnigan, Ty Martin, and Gene Smith for their assistance in producing the first edition, to Donald Graves and Donald Hickey for commenting on the original text, and to Gemma Gardner and her colleagues at Osprey for shepherding the manuscript through to an attractive second edition. I also thank the public institutions that promote historical understanding through freely sharing period images from their collections for publication, especially the Houghton, John Carter Brown, and William L. Clements libraries, the McCord Stewart, Metropolitan, and Smithsonian museums, the Library of Congress, Washington's National Gallery of Art and National Portrait Gallery, and the Yale University Art Gallery.

Image notes

The full credit line for the image on page 4 is Harris Brisbane Dick Fund, 1964

The full credit line for the image on page 14 is The Edward W. C. Arnold Collection of New York Prints, Maps and Pictures, Bequest of Edward W. C. Arnold, 1954

The image on page 19 can be found at: https://npg.si.edu/object/npg_NPG.82.71

The images on page 20, 41 and 82 are available under CC BY-SA 4.0: https://creativecommons.org/licenses/by-sa/4.0/

The image on page 93 can be found at: https://npg.si.edu/object/npg_NPG.2013.139

INDEX